**"**

I SAW WONDERS.
I GOBBLED UP THE SCENERY,
I ATE WELL, SLEPT WELL AND
I LEARNT A LOT: FROM THE
AMBITIONS OF EDWARD I TO THE
APPETITES OF THE DUNG BEETLE.
WHAT A COUNTRY, WHAT VARIETY,
WHAT PEOPLE.

**"**

# GRIFF RHYS JONES

## INSUFFICIENTLY WELSH

# PARTHIAN

**PARTHIAN**
The Old Surgery
Napier Street
Cardigan
SA43 1ED

www.parthianbooks.com

First published in 2014
© Griff Rhys Jones/Modern TV 2014
All Rights Reserved
ISBN 9781909844995

**EDITOR**
Francesca Rhydderch

**PHOTOGRAPHY**
Scott Dewey

**DESIGN / TYPESETTING**
Marc Jennings - www.theundercard.co.uk

Printed and bound by Gomer Press, Llandysul, Wales

Published with the financial support of the Welsh Books Council

British Library Cataloguing in Publication Data
A cataloguing record for this book is available from the British Library.

# – INTRODUCTION –

Over the years I have learned to "swallow the toad". It's not a Welsh expression. Nice if it was. I got it from Sicily, via Norman Lewis, the master travel writer (Welsh himself, actually, now I come to think of it). Was Lewis perhaps a little prone to "embroidery"? Is that perhaps a Welsh romantic trait? I am getting ahead of myself. I can't start off with wild racial generalisations; there's plenty of time for that later. I just like the phrase. It has resonance.

For my part, the toads I have gulped down, straight-faced, include the rejection of virtually every programme idea I have ever proposed to television executives since 1990. I have ingested Catanian swamps of wart-ridden amphibious reptiles, in brown offices in ugly buildings. But this one lingers. It was my "Monkey Tennis". Ten years ago, I went to a BBC Wales "commissioner" and proposed a televisual entertainment featuring a well-known British television star. I thought this celebrity would add some lustre to BBC Wales's output – and I could get him cheap.

There was a sickly pause. I detected what might best be described as a shudder. "No…" he opined, with a wonderful Welsh open-vowelled negative. He was about to present a toad for my delectation, I could tell. "Not him. No. I am afraid he would be insufficiently Welsh."

My face was a standing stone. It was useless to point out that my presenter was funny, beloved, celebrated and starry – and a personal friend of mine as well. Pointless to enquire whether Welsh television viewers might enjoy a less parochial presenter. Silly to point out that Wales can cope with outsiders, just as the English embrace Terry Wogan, Gavin Esler and er… Huw Edwards.

I swallowed manfully. "Yes, of course," I said.

Something dark flopped into my belly.

I realised, however, as I stared into the glassy eye of my interlocutor, that there was a subtext to our conversation. You see, it was not really my proposal that was insufficiently Welsh, or my mate. It was something else. The commissioner was gazing steadily at Griffith Rhys Jones, son of Elwyn and Gwynneth, scion of Megan and Ieuan and Evan, spawn of Betws-y-Coed, Penmachno and the Rhondda, Cardiff-born, dark of hair, thick-thighed and round-faced. And I suspected that he thought that it was me who was insufficiently Welsh.

Having been brought up in London (founded by a Welshman, according to legend), one of the Essex Boyos, a white-wellington booted Dragon at the end of the Central line and having missed the cultural communal Celtic after-game warm bath of Cymric fellow-feeling, who did I think I was, returning to Cardiff and pretending to have connections?

So, am I insufficiently Welsh? It's time to find out. That is what this book is all about. I am going out on the road to search for my Celtic roots and explore "the land of my aunties". Language, the landscape, rugby, dogs, legends, botany, wildlife, furniture and a few more bits on the side: I looked into them all and here are the results.

***

Just to book-end here, though: a little while later I had another suggestion for BBC Wales. This time they were looking for a satirical show. I have made a few anarchic sallies in the past. A prominent politician had become annoyed with the election results in the principality and vented his frustration in public. We suggested a hard-hitting riposte called "The Fucking Welsh".

We didn't even get asked to an interview on that one.

# – A BIT OF BACKGROUND –

My father used the telephone as if announcing a concert party on a pre-war radio. If he could ever be persuaded to answer the thing, and then only in the absence of my mother, whose delegated task this normally was, he lifted the heavy, black, Bakelite lump from its cradle in the hallway, straightened his back and addressed the caller as if from the other side of a canyon. "Hellooo?" He would declare. "Who am I speaking with?"

His usual faux home-counties tones would swoop into a musical lilt. (And he was no musician.) There was immediately a pronounced fruitiness to his vocal chords. We were back in the Valleys. My father became Welsh on the telephone, God bless him.

"The Valleys"? Ah, but here I show my own ignorance. We were Welsh alright. My mother came from Ferndale, in the Rhondda – which is, I believe, a proper valley. My father emerged from a gloomy red house in the suburbs of Cardiff. (This was more of "a slight hill" than a valley.) Every single relative I have seems to have been vehemently Welsh, but I do not mean that they came from "the Valleys". I am making wild, clichéd outsider generalities already.

Elwyn's was the posh voice of the Cardiff suburbs, of the lawyers and physicians of the great coal port. Their inclination was to be Saxon in their manners. I was born in Cardiff but we moved away when I was six months old. I left a legion of aunties and great aunties, grannies and nans encamped across the lower west from Tonypandy to Pontypridd. It gave us our identity, in English Epping. We had to watch the rugby. I was dragooned into the choir. Sometimes we went to Dagenham to visit fellow Welsh exile doctors, who smoked and cackled a lot and had an easy, soppy familiarity that I came to associate with proper comfortable Welshness.

My granny and grandpa moved to join us. He had been a miner and wore a cloth cap and swore impressively in pidgin Welsh, as he levered his wheezing and arthritic body into the Morris Traveller. ("Duw, duw, oh fucky!" - "Grandpa!! The children!!") Granny wrote letters in Welsh to Aunty Betty. There were Megans and Ieuans, Wyns, Gwens, Gwynneths, Gwyns and Evanses all over the Christmas card list.

"You must have experienced a lot of racial prejudice, growing up in Epping." One Welsh actor had taken me aside, when we worked together on Russell T Davies's *Mine all Mine* for ITV drama.

I wondered what he was on about. "No, not really," I started carefully. "Nobody ever really noticed I was Welsh."

He nodded sagely. "That's exactly what I mean." He looked sorrowful. "They don't care about the Welsh, you see – the English."

In all honesty, nobody did care that I was Welsh. I am not really included in Wales by the Welsh. How could I be, with my weird part Essex tough junior school, part posh Sussex kindergarten accent? Mavis Nicholson once disparaged me to my face for speaking with a "pretentious" voice. (Oh, for your common touch, Mavis, love.)

I often went to Wales when I was tiny, by the long one-way system that went through every traffic light in Britain. In Cardiff we stayed with the forbidding Nain (North Walian Welsh for Nan). She was a tall woman with a shock of long, long white hair, tied up in a bun, attended throughout her life by my spinster Auntie Megan, who had big teeth and spaniel eyes. They had no idea when we might arrive, so they never cooked. Wales meant imprisonment for hours in that Morris Traveller and then salad: ham and hard-boiled eggs, and I hated salad. Cardiff meant the arcades ("What's so good about them, Granny?"). It meant walking with excruciatingly slow ancient people. It meant loud ticking clocks in dark drawing rooms, and being on my best behaviour.

As I grew older, I kept away. The relatives all died. I went to visit my elderly uncle, who dressed like Edward VIII, spent a great deal of time in the South of France and was the only person I ever met who said "…what?" at the end of sentences, like a character in a Wodehouse story. ("Splendid day, what?") But even he once sat me down in his pink wallpapered modern house near Radyr golf course and gently upbraided me. "You don't want to make fun of Wales in those sketches of yours, what?"

Yes, even this dandy, with his Mr. Fish shirts and his Meissen candlesticks and his sports cars and snuffly pug dogs was a patriotic, full-blooded Welshman under the plus fours. (I still have those plus fours. He really wore them.)

The realisation took me aback. Because, like all of us, I have been fed the clichés. I know the Welshness of coal mines and choirs. What Londoner does not? But Wales is surely much more than truncated witches' hats and bardic chairs, though even those have their fascination. (And indeed for years we had a proper Welsh hat in a box in a proper Welsh coffer in our Epping front room.)

When I threw off the shackles of my yearly sketch show and was given a new life in television, as a middle-aged man going "Oh, how beautiful" in scenic travelogues, I was taken beyond Cardiff. I started to range about the Principality. I climbed mountains and I canoed rivers, I walked sea fronts, and plunged into valleys, I went from the noisy, crowded cities to what, I finally understood, were the most remote and beautiful places in Britain.

I got to further understand Wales's geography and its size, but always in hurried, speedy chunks, as we rattled from Conwy to Fishguard, or into the Black Hills for a quick photo opportunity. *Restoration* took me to look at some extraordinary houses. *Who Do you Think You Are* sat me down in Carmarthen High Court. *Mine All Mine* showed me Gower. Eventually, I became totally rootsy and bought a small patch of land and a ruined farmhouse on the wild and unearthly coast of Pembrokeshire.

But it is time to take stock. There is no one totality called Wales. There are many distinct regions in this small country. There are huge variations in geography and landscape. There are hidden wonders and strange attractions. There are unexpected cosmopolitan touches and eccentric ambitions.

Instead of waking up to eat salad and then going straight to bed, on this visit to Wales I intend to linger and explore and find out what is distinctive, so I am visiting eight separate regions and looking around – not to be comprehensive (the journeys are often deliberately small-scale) – but to get closer. And for each separate chapter in this odyssey I am tying together a loose knot. I have a mission to fulfil, a quest to pursue. Like an errant knight I have a given goal. It is designed to release the Welshness in me. Will I get closer to Cymru through my "challenges"? I hope so.

–1–

# MONMOUTHSHIRE

## THE GREAT BARRIER

MONMOUTHSHIRE | THE GREAT BARRIER | 08

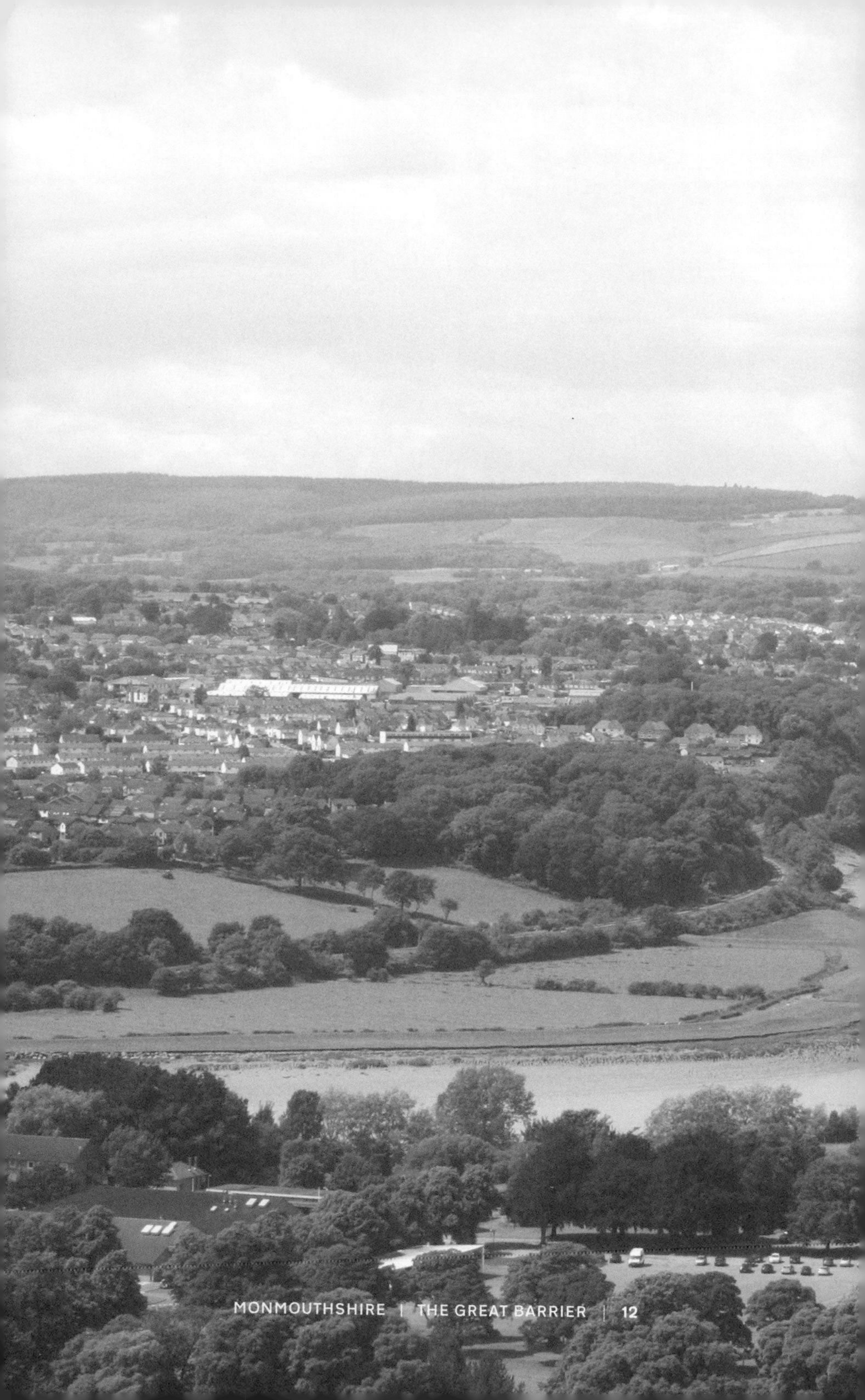

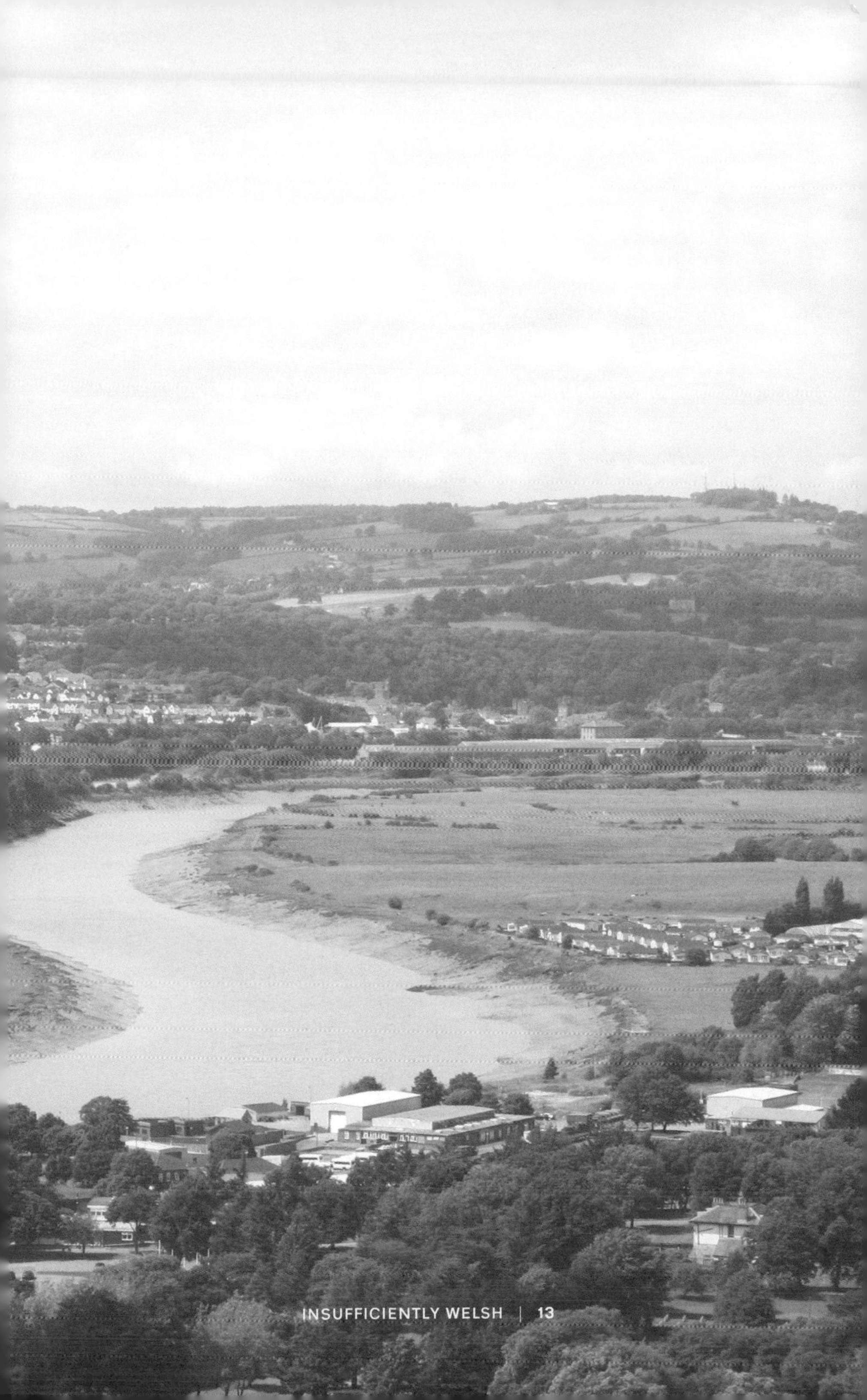

Have I ever been this way before?

The thought came to me as we walked down through a reed bed, at the end of a deserted roadway, towards salt marshes and a muddy foreshore, to confront the remnants of a former passenger terminal in a crumbling block overgrown with brambles. It smelled, in that suspicious way that abandoned breeze-block buildings do, but the turnstiles were rusted up so we climbed through a hole in the fence.

Ahead was the mighty Severn, like a wide, flat, grey sinister pond. Downstream, towards the sea-horizon, (which I have never seen blue, only muddy and dismal) was the new bridge, soaring into the air between its lengthy jetties. Upstream was its far more handsome older brother. This elegant, white, full-span crossing was built in the early sixties. It put to an end the business of the ferry point where I was now standing.

From 1926 the Aust ferry had been the old posh car route. For a car and driver in 1955, it cost four shillings to cross into Wales. It had to be profitable for the owners; so much so, that it is said that a hearse using the crossing was invoiced a further one shilling and six pence for the coffin.

The kids from the village used to gather to watch the popstars go through. The famous photograph of Bob Dylan (and that Phantom Rolls Royce as black as his hair) was taken, not in some Mississippi Delta, but right here on this foreshore, when those shaggy stumps in front of me supported wooden planks that made a landing stage. The Aust crossing was notorious. Daniel Defoe, the author of *Robinson Crusoe*, was deterred from using it because of the risk, describing it as "an ugly, dangerous, and very inconvenient ferry".

I rang my mother. "Did we ever come this way?" I asked. I reckoned that by 1960 I was seven. I was living in Sussex. And we might have got to Cardiff via this route, but she quickly dashed that fantasy.

"No, we never took a ferry," she told me. "We must have gone via Gloucester."

"Or Chepstow?" I suggested.

"Possibly. I can't remember, darling."

I was already more sentimental about Wales and my Welshness than my mother ever wanted to be. At 89, Gwynneth has no nostalgia for the land of her fathers. I was the one floundering in the past.

But as I turned to go the land of my fathers went with me. My "challenge", my quest (what I had to do this section of the trip), had been stuck in a cleft in a particularly soggy rotten jetty post on the other side of an eel-grass bog. I took my new suede walking boots for a trial in the estuary mud and ended up clutching an instruction. It was "to perform the National Anthem in Welsh".

Fair enough. I might seek to avoid an incipient John Redwood catastrophe. No miming for me. I knew the tune. I knew the sentiment and, indeed most of the words in English, but the Welsh element would be a definite step up.

Germaine Greer (if I can just name-drop indiscriminately and, I think, impressively) once explained to me that the reason we English speakers struggle with Welsh is its orthography. Sixth-century Welsh documents use Latin characters, but there are many extra sounds to cope with. These were already represented by new letters in the alphabet. This means there are 28 letters in the Welsh alphabet, which comprises of seven vowels and twenty one consonants. "Ll" is one letter in Welsh and two in English. So there are six letters in Llanelli, if you are Welsh, and eight if you are English. Early transcribers of the language needed to represent a greater range of sounds. "W"s become "oos". "U"s are in fact like double "i"s. "F" is a "v" and so forth. The "ch" sound was originally represented by a "k", but the printers of the Welsh Bible didn't have enough "k"s so they moved on to "c"s and the "k" fell out of use altogether.

Welsh was the first language of us Britons. You are reading here, on this page, a more recent immigrant, bastard hybrid – English. Welsh is one of the oldest languages still spoken in Europe and until 1911 Welsh was still the majority language in Wales. Today about half a million people in Wales can speak Welsh. In 1911 it was nearly double that.

The river that I was now skirting was defined as a barrier during the reign of Athelstan in 926, who ordered that the Britons, the older inhabitants of these islands, should stay to the west and the Saxons to the east. Matters of a national and patriarchal identity have been an issue for over a thousand years, especially at this very gateway to Wales. But I wonder if language is the real barrier. And the real identity of Wales.

I tried to master some Welsh a few years back. I was renovating a house in Pembrokeshire and I thought I would need the Welsh language to banter with the builders. Alas, it transpired they all came from Essex, like me. Although several surveys commissioned by S4C (the Welsh-language TV channel) have suggested that there are around 200,000

Welsh speakers living in England, none of the builders were part of this so I left it.

It is superficially difficult. Double "d"s, double "l"s, guttural noises and consonants are yoked together to make distinct and seemingly unnatural traps for the English speaker. But everybody tells me that it is easy. "At least Welsh is spelled as it is pronounced," I was told. "You just have to speak the letters as they appear."

So I wanted to start with something simple and the anthem seemed a good choice. I had after ten years mastered road instructions. *Araf,* (with a v sound at the end). That meant slow. *Parcio* meant "parking". When I first crossed the Severn Bridge with my wife, I pointed out that the Welsh began straightaway. "Look there," I said, pointing to a toll sign. "Manned!" I pronounced it as "manneth". What does that mean?

"It means there's a man to serve you in that booth. It's in English."


## – FOOTBRIDGE –

There wasn't a booth to get onto the bridge if you were walking. Three hundred million cars have driven over since it was opened; at least half as many seemed to be thundering past now.

It took three-and-a-half years to build the thing, at a cost of £8 million. Upon opening it in 1966, the Queen hailed it as "the dawn of a new economic era for south Wales" and it was far more emphatic and sculptural than the later rival, further south, which wanders out on a raised platform across the shallows for several miles before it deigns to raise towers and hang a short traverse. White, pure, simple, elegant: the original Severn Bridge is a confident, sixties, geometric design. Like a piece of origami, or a white plastic egg chair, it epitomises groovy pop Britain and now has Grade I listed status.

Each section of deck was made in Chepstow and floated into position, before being hauled into the sky. Seen close up, however, like many roadways or bits of plant, it seemed gritty, noisy and alien. Solitary human beings are not meant to grapple with this sort of engineering. We had to invent superheroes to hold on to broken cables or fly underneath suspension bridges, or tip cars into the river. It is not for mere mortals.

As I strolled along, first one bicycle whizzed by and then another. They

# AUST FERRY

IT IS BELIEVED THAT THE FERRY DATES BACK TO ROMAN TIMES, WHEN THEY USED A FERRY FROM THIS POINT TO TRANSPORT LEGIONS ACROSS TO WALES.

---

THE STONE PIERS USED BY THE FERRY WERE BUILT IN 1825 BY THE LORDS OF TIDENHAM WHO OWNED THE PASSAGE RIGHTS BETWEEN THE 12TH AND 19TH CENTURIES.

---

IT WAS SUCH A DANGEROUS CROSSING THAT IN 1839 ONE OF THE FERRIES WAS LOST TO THE WATERS. THERE WERE NO SURVIVORS. THE SAME THING HAPPENED AGAIN IN 1844.

---

IN 1955 FOR A PASSENGER TO CROSS ON THE FERRY IT COST ONE SHILLING, FOR A CAR AND ITS DRIVER IT COST FOUR SHILLINGS.

---

WHEN THE WEATHER WAS FAVOURABLE IT WOULD TAKE 12 MINUTES TO CROSS THE SEVERN ON THE FERRY

---

THE FERRY COULD HOLD BETWEEN 17 AND 19 CARS AND NEARLY 100 PASSENGERS.

---

THE MARTIN SCORSESE FILM 'NO DIRECTION HOME' ABOUT THE LIFE OF BOB DYLAN HAS A PROMOTIONAL SHOT OF DYLAN STANDING IN FRONT OF THE AUST FERRY TERMINAL IN MAY 1966, JUST FOUR MONTHS BEFORE THE FERRY CLOSED FOR GOOD.

---

LOCALS TELL STORIES OF HOW SCHOOL CHILDREN WOULD RUSH TO THE RIVER FERRY TO GLIMPSE STARS LIKE THE BEATLES AND TOM JONES ON THEIR WAY TO PERFORM IN WALES.

looked surprised to see me walking there at all. I had noticed dozens of cars parked haphazardly up on verges in the bushy lanes surrounding the approach road. "They park on one side or the other," a bridge engineer called Paul told me. "Six quid toll. It mounts up every day, so they bike across for free."

The toll is collected "on the English side," as the old complaint has it. It's free to get out of Wales. You pay to go in. (Quite right too, because from the very outset Wales offers up her beauties. We should pay. I mean you should pay.)

Paul and I took a lift up, through the box structure, to the top of the tower, to get a look into the Welsh heartland from a superlative viewing platform. The prospect defined Wales, because even from a height of 445 feet my view ahead was already blocked by rising hills. The Land of my Fathers becomes the Hillside that keeps a Welcome and the Valley that is unquestionably Green almost immediately.

My eyes, however, were hardly fixed on the distant horizon; they kept being drawn back to what lies beneath. The car deck had shrunk to become a sliver of road, traversed by models. Below that, a swathe of dirty water spread in the feathered patterns of great tidal movements. We felt high: too high not to automatically reach for a handrail for security.

"This first bridge was the more expensive bridge," Paul was explaining as he leaned down and started to tackle me up. "It was aerodynamically designed and no expense was spared." He was reaching around under my arms and attaching a colossal safety belt. "But the other one was safer. Eleven men died building this thing. One fell off into the concrete mixer and they never got him out, so now we take safety very seriously indeed."

Soon there were four supports dangling from my harness. Two were long, two short and all of them ended in a big clip shackle. The thing felt as cumbersome as a suit of armour.

"Of course, the oldest crossing is the tunnel. That runs out there." He pointed to the water by the other bridge as he took me by the arm. "That was Brunel's great achievement. It remains in use but it still floods. They hit a spring and they had to pump out the water. They still do. It's used to make beer."

We were now standing by the northern cable. The bridge is literally suspended. The main cables are each made up of 8,322 individual 5mm wires. It needs constant monitoring by a team of experts who simply walk out onto it to make their inspections.

"It's steepest up here and gets flatter as you go along. You might basically continue your walk right the way down it and into Wales," Paul laughed. "Except you wouldn't be in Wales at all. Despite having crossed the Severn Bridge, you are still in England." He pointed to another smaller suspension bridge that finished the crossing. "That's the Wye Bridge," he explained.

And for the first time, despite having travelled both the Wye and the Severn, I realised that the bridge actually crossed both rivers just before they join together. Ironically, these rivers begin life within a hundred yards of each other up in the Plynlimon Mountains behind Aberystwyth. They take widely separate trajectories to meet again in tidal waters.

Paul was joking about the walk down, but he was not joking about a stroll on the cable. My task now was to saunter out and follow some of the engineers on an inspection.

I have no particular fear of heights. I have abseiled off skyscrapers, my dears. Only three times in my life have I ever been overcome by vertigo. The first time was when I was hauled up a ship's mast. The second time was on a snow-covered ridge on Suilven, in the far north of Scotland. This was the third.

My guide went ahead and I was invited to follow. There were two hand rails. My shackles and supporting lines were attached to rails on both sides. But the cable, on which I tentatively put my foot, was spherical, encased as it was in a metal protective sheath. I immediately felt that I might slip off it. But I couldn't slip. I mustn't slip.

This sheathing seemed insecure as a footfall. There was no reason for that insecurity. It was a big, fat, round thing, about three foot across I reckoned. But that made it worse. And it sloped down. That made it untenable.

I was wearing my new walking boots, still flecked with estuary mud. They seemed clod-hopping and clumsy. My feet now shrank inside them to become amoeba feet. They felt unable to connect with any surface. I stared at them, willing them to move on, but the problem was clear. Beyond my feet I was looking directly downwards onto the miniature deck, hundreds of feet below, swarming with hurrying, tiny cars, and below that, to compound the sense of height, the tide itself, swirling and gyrating.

Oh God. I was far less at risk than if I had stood on a coffee table. If I slipped, the support belts would certainly hold me, but I could not seem to convince my brain, my subconscious or my mortal self of that fact.

The idea was that I would help carry out an inspection by squatting down and unscrewing a plate. Now I was talking slowly and they could all hear the hollow cadence in my voice.

I looked up. My guide had a puzzled frown. It wasn't lifting the inspection hatch that concerned him. He was wondering what he would do if I froze into a blob of iced panic jelly. So I laughed. A big mistake, because now I sounded positively maniacal too, and I stepped forward. That felt terrible. It got no better. The cable was steady. The wind was light. I was terrified.

We probably went no further than ten yards down and out, over yawning space. I pretended to be interested in the inspection hatch. Then they turned me around, by releasing each of my retention straps and re-connecting them one by one. I mechanically forced my arm to twist over and grip the other side of the rail before I tiptoed my way back to the platform.

Having got there and gripped the railing I turned and smiled wanly at the guys who gambolled about on that tube on a daily basis. They smiled back.

## – DYKE STUFF –

The bridges and tunnels are a modern gateway to Wales: a conquest of the muddy sluice of the Severn. A little way up the west bank, however, but still in England, I went in search of older, longer and cruder civil engineering: a monument to something far more mysterious – vanity, power or paranoia: you choose. I was startled to find that we don't really know what Offa's Dyke really is.

For a start it is less a dyke than a rampart.

Beginning in a little grove of trees, on the top of a cliff, a substantial wall of earth (with a well-trodden path on top of it) snaked away to the north. I have walked in "Boudicca's encampment" in the middle of Epping Forest. I have stood on the raised humps of many Iron Age forts. Though dating from a similarly foggy period, this was a bigger deal than any of those minor wrinkles in the carpet.

Jim Saunders, the Offa's Dyke path officer for nearly 20 years, joined me some ten feet above the surrounding fields. Had we wanted to, we could have followed the rampart for about 150 miles to Prestatyn (or perhaps to the Dee Estuary). There is some dispute as to whether the

# SEVERN BRIDGES

8,000 TONS OF STEEL WERE USED IN THE
CONSTRUCTION OF THE ORIGINAL BRIDGE.

---

IT WAS ONCE BELIEVED THERE WAS A CHEST
OF GOLD BURIED UNDER THE SEVERN, WHICH
LED TO MANY PEOPLE DIGGING IN THE AREA
IN 1878.

---

AT HIGH WATER THE RIVER SEVERN IS NEARLY
EXACTLY ONE MILE WIDE AT THE POINT WHERE THE
SEVERN BRIDGE IS LOCATED.

---

ONE OF THE REASONS THAT THE SECOND SEVERN
CROSSING WAS BUILT WAS BECAUSE BETWEEN
1980 AND 1990 TRAFFIC FLOWS ON THE SEVERN
BRIDGE INCREASED BY 63%.

---

THE OVERALL LENGTH OF THE NEW SEVERN
BRIDGE EXCEEDS 5000M, MAKING IT ONE
OF THE LONGEST SUSPENSION BRIDGES
IN THE WORLD.

---

ABOUT 80,000 VEHICLES CROSS THE TWO
BRIDGES EVERY DAY.

---

PLANS TO BUILD A BARRAGE TO HARNESS
HYDROELECTRICITY HAVE BEEN PROPOSED
SINCE AS EARLY AS THE 1960s.

whole ditch and wall should be attributed to Offa, and archaeologists have argued about which bit of dyke was built when, but it is indisputable that here is the longest ancient monument in Britain and possibly even Europe, and one about which almost nothing can be ascertained.

Offa, a "vigorous" powerful Christian king, ruled most of southern England between 757 and 796AD. He seems to have subdued East Anglia and sorted out Kent. There are fine coins with his bulbous face on them. George Borrow, in his classic, *Wild Wales*, noted that at one time "it was customary for the English to cut off the ears of every Welshman who was found to the east of the dyke, and for the Welsh to hang every Englishman whom they found to the west of it". These are most likely fictions, but this rampart certainly has its ditch on the Welsh side. It also skirts around the western side of any hills, so it seems that people on the wall were able to look out into Wales... for what purpose? Welsh marauders, invaders or sheep-stealers, one supposes, possibly erroneously.

Offa certainly fought campaigns against the Welsh in 778, 784 and 796. But revisionist historians have decided that the dyke might be a giant vanity project. "You want to know how big and powerful a king I am, then look on my mighty mud heap and despair."

As Jim and I lumbered up hills and down into valleys, watched by curious cows, warbling birds and a camera crew, I could only marvel at this manmade lump. I know from bitter personal experience that the most expensive hobby in the world is neither horse racing nor yachting but landscaping.

They planned to build the Severn Bridge just after the war and finally got it done twenty years later. By all accounts, or, let's be strictly accurate, by one account, given by Asser and written 200 years after the event in his "History of Alfred the Great", they knocked this wall up in a similar stretch of time, using leather buckets, 1300 years ago.

Or maybe not. My mind was already more boggled by this ditch than it had been by the view from the top of the bridge. And now I wanted to follow it all the way to Prestatyn, crossing back and forth with it in and out of Wales as we went. But I had to leave. I was supposed to be exploring the Land of My Fathers (and singing it), and I hadn't even got into the country yet.

# - WELSH CHEPSTOW -

I took the fine 1816 cast-iron bridge and crossed into Chepstow and thus into Wales, wondering how Welsh this border town really could be. "Welsh enough for the inhabitants to pass the other way to get a drink in England on Sunday nights not so long ago," I was told by Ivor, whom I met on the waterfront.

What a strange outlook we had too. We sat on a bench on the quayside, gazing across at an English limestone cliff with a Union Jack painted, provocatively, halfway up a stone face, next to a reputed smuggler's cave. Ivor pointed out that it was now occupied as a vantage point by a pair of breeding ospreys, who sat watching us watching them. The River Wye trickled along somewhere deep below us in a gut, waiting for the tide to rise in a mad bath of muddy water and bring its surface up to where we were sitting.

Despite the empty channel, Chepstow was the biggest port in Wales in medieval times, renowned for the importation of wine and the exportation of timber and bark from the nearby Wye valley and the Forest of Dean. Clinging to the pinnacle of another cliff to the left was William FitzOsbern's castle: an English toehold in Wales and often cited as the oldest surviving stone castle in Britain. It is a symbol of the Norman appetite for conquest. This was "Marcher" country. The threat of "border trouble" meant that extra powers were given to families like the Bigods, who then became so mighty that it took centuries to bring them back under control.

Monmouthshire became a non-partisan land. It was left out of Henry VIII's reforming laws of Wales so it remained partly attached to England. When they required higher justice, its inhabitants had to appeal to the Old Bailey, not to Carmarthen, and it was only as recently as 1974 that it officially became part of Wales. So one might assume that its population would gravitate towards England. Apparently not. They fall to Wales. In Chepstow people take their Welshness seriously, including the language. Ivor himself was learning Welsh.

He took me along to his class, meeting in the gatehouse of the town and attended by people of all ages and sexes. Perhaps I would be able to sort out some of my difficulties with the National Anthem.

# CHEPSTOW

POPULATION: 12,350 (2011 CENSUS).

IN MEDIEVAL TIMES, CHEPSTOW WAS THE
LARGEST PORT IN WALES; ITS SHIPS SAILED
AS FAR AS ICELAND AND TURKEY.

OTTER HOLE CAVE IN CHEPSTOW IS ONE OF
THE LONGEST CAVE SYSTEMS IN BRITAIN.

CHEPSTOW WAS ONCE THE MOST IMPORTANT
TOWN IN WALES, BUT BY THE 1880s
IT NO LONGER HAD CUSTOMS FACILITIES
TO COMPETE WITH GROWING COAL PORTS
LIKE CARDIFF AND SWANSEA.

ONE OF THE FIRST WORLD WAR SHIPYARDS
WAS ESTABLISHED IN CHEPSTOW.

DURING WORLD WAR II CHEPSTOW RACECOURSE
ESSENTIALITY BECAME RAF CHEPSTOW, WITH THE
GREEN SPACE IN THE MIDDLE OF THE TRACK BEING
USED AS A RUNWAY.

CHEPSTOW'S TUBULAR RAILWAY BRIDGE
WAS DESIGNED BY BRUNEL IN 1852.

# – LAND OF MY DIPTHONGS –

"Chhh!" We began with sounds. My Aunty Megan used to chide me for saying Welsh was difficult. "Bach" with that extra "ccchhh". Like hawking. My Dad called me "Griffith Bach" when I frustrated him, as I so often did. It has that guttural noise that we Saxon-educated outsiders can't get used to.

In fact everybody Welsh seems to chide me for finding it difficult. Tudor, the cameraman, and Brian on sound chided me for finding it difficult. Celyn, the assistant producer, chided me and it was her mother Heulwen doing the teaching now.

"Stick your tongue up against your teeth and blow through it."

"Lllll."

"Now you can say Llanelli".

And I could. In 1977 the Voyager satellite was sent up to space in search of intelligent life with greetings in 55 different languages, one of which was Welsh.

Research suggests that there are as many as 750,000 Welsh speakers in the world. I am not even close.

I once went to Conwy to round up some wild ponies and the farmer greeted me with enthusiasm. "Well, Griffith Rhys" he said, "I'm a Rhys myself. Don't you just hate it when people pronounce your name wrong." I nodded vacantly, suddenly conscious that I must have been pronouncing my own name wrong for my entire life.

There is an "h" in there, you see, and the Welsh hit every part of the true spelling, so that it can be heard. It's not Rees or Rice, it's R-hees. I spend hours trying to master the right rolling "arr" followed by the distinct click of the "h" and I never managed it without stumbling over my own teeth.

But here I am again, willing, but frankly too old to turn on the sixpence in my own gob. "Gwlad…" we sing in the anthem. "In fact we sing it again, to give it extra emphasis. "Gwlad".

"And its not a "you" or a "double you", it's an "oo", but hatefully it looks like "glad" so my fuzzy brain still keeps trying to make it sound like that. I have a long way to go. And I feel dismal. At my age, did I have the capacity to learn the language of my fathers? That could be discovered. But did I have the will? That was a more complicated proposition.

# WELSH LANGUAGE

THERE ARE 28 LETTERS IN THE WELSH ALPHABET, 7 VOWELS AND 21 CONSONANTS.

IN 1536 THE PASSING OF THE 'ACT OF UNION' OF HENRY VIII PROHIBITED THE USE OF WELSH IN PUBLIC ADMINISTRATION AND THE LEGAL SYSTEM.

IN THE SIXTH CENTURY WELSH WAS SPOKEN IN MOST OF BRITAIN, INCLUDING STRATHCLYDE IN SCOTLAND, WHICH IS DERIVED FROM ITS FORMER WELSH NAME. SOME SHEPHERDS IN CUMBRIA WERE STILL COUNTING THEIR SHEEP IN WELSH IN THE TWENTIETH CENTURY.

THE 1911 CENSUS RECORDED THE HIGHEST NUMBER OF WELSH SPEAKERS – 977,366. IT ALSO REVEALED THAT THE WELSH LANGUAGE HAD, FOR THE FIRST TIME, BECOME A MINORITY LANGUAGE, SPOKEN BY 43.5% OF THE POPULATION.

IN 1939 THE FIRST PRIVATE WELSH LANGUAGE SCHOOL WAS ESTABLISHED IN ABERYSTWYTH.

IN 1942 THE WELSH COURTS ACT ESTABLISHED LIMITED RIGHTS TO USE THE WELSH LANGUAGE IN A COURT OF LAW FOR THE FIRST TIME SINCE 1536.

IN 1947 WELSH MEDIUM SCHOOL YSGOL GYMRAEG LLANELLI OPENED. THIS WAS THE FIRST DESIGNATED WELSH MEDIUM SCHOOL TO BE FULLY MAINTAINED BY AN EDUCATION AUTHORITY.

# – WITH A PADDLE –

Canoeing was an easier skill to master, but we had to catch the tide. The brown sludge at the base of the canyon, beneath the flange of mud, below the bank of bilious salt marsh, had started boiling and frothing northwards just after lunch. With almost 50 feet of tidal difference between low and high tide, that flood had once brought old sailing ships shooting up the estuary (and beyond for another five miles) and we needed to catch it.

I have canoed on the Wye before. (Here we are, going round in circles again.) In the programme "Rivers", we came south on what was voted the nation's favorite river in 2010. I learned to kayak and shoot rapids near Ross. Now we formed a posse intent on going the other way.

We manhandled the long canoes over the wall at the edge of the quay, slid them down the grab-rails on top of a bridge to a pontoon and plopped them into the water.

"Avoid the buoys," Graham told me. He pointed. The flow was so strong that it dragged these obstacles half-under and rendered them almost invisible. We were four in separate vessels. I knelt forward on my haunches, wedged my bum against the little rattan seat and pushed out into the coffee-coloured stream.

We were quickly swept away. The tide shot us under the bridge and past the castle and soon we were following what had once been Britain's first tourist route.

Excited by the renown of the scenery and the philosophy of "the picturesque", packages of eighteenth-century aesthetes had followed a trail of wonders identified for them by William Gilpin. Their routes were carefully organised to allow them to see specific sites, sites which, if caught at exactly the right angle, even contained within portable frames, presented the composition and proportions of a proper picture. That was the point. Nature was at its best if organised. We were less fussy. We just paddled and gawped.

"It's still a canoeing mecca for enthusiasts from all over Europe", Graham told me.

Tourists had been drifting up and down this famous river for centuries and yet, around the bend from Chepstow, we seemed to drop into the Canadian outback. The river was unspoilt. The Welsh side rose up in a sharp cliff, smothered in mature trees, a tapestry of contrasting greens on this sunny July day. On the English side, a few dun cows grazed in a meadow.

A gentle poke with my paddle kept me on course, past water meadows and overhanging alders. Graham, my guide, had first taken me kayaking ten years before. He had stood high on a bank and watched me paddle into Ross-on-Wye and told my assistant that I was doing it wrong.

My assistant, with considerable glee, promptly told me, "You're doing it all wrong, you know."

I didn't. Up to that point I had no idea there was a right way and wrong way to paddle.

Subsequently I have been instructed and inspected. But I like to paddle on both sides. One paddle on one side: dip and pull. Then across over to the other side: dip and pull. It always seemed natural to me. Like rowing, you control your pace and direction with opposing strokes. But I shouldn't do that. A proper canoeist squats down and paddles on one side only, steering the course by feathering the paddle.

It worries me to be with canoeists who do it correctly because I think they probably think I am a dork, so I remember to do it right for a bit, and then do it wrong for a bit and the pleasure that I once took in canoeing is entirely gone.

The river was lovely, though.

## – A LOAD OF BELLS –

We landed back in England, opposite the ruins of Tintern Abbey, slithering up the steep bank between overgrown reeds. I had to cross back by another handsome steel bridge and I was in Wales again.

I had been singing while tramping, and I set off across a meadow now, bellowing out what I could remember of the national anthem. I had been supplied with a phonetic version.

> My hen oo-lad vurr n'had-die un ann-wil ee mee
> goo-lard bay-rdd a chann-tor-eon
> enn wog eon o vree
> ane goo-rol ruvv-el-weir
> goo-lard gar-weir tra mard
> dross rudd-id cor-llar-sant ay goo-eyed.

Any use? Well yes, up to a point. It doesn't really seem to fit the music. It was also more confusing than the written Welsh. And that real, written

# WYE FACTS

THE WYE DRAINS A TOTAL CATCHMENT
AREA OF 4,200 SQ KM.

---

THE RIVER WYE IS PART OF A 5-PART SYSTEM
OF STREAMS INCLUDING THE GWY, HAFRON,
RHEIDOL AND THE SEVERN. AN OLD WELSH FOLK
STORY TELLS THE TALE OF THESE FIVE 'DAUGHTERS'
AND THEIR JOURNEYS TO THE SEA.

---

IN 1607 THERE WAS A GREAT FLOOD THAT
SOME CALLED A TSUNAMI, WHERE 2000 PEOPLE
DROWNED IN MONMOUTHSHIRE.

---

HISTORICALLY THE WYE WAS AN IMPORTANT
TRANSPORT LINK FOR INDUSTRY IN THE 1800s.

---

MORE THAN 30 SPECIES OF FISH HAVE BEEN
RECORDED IN THE WYE, MAKING IT ONE OF
THE MOST IMPORTANT RIVER SYSTEMS IN
NORTHERN EUROPE.

---

IN THE RIVER WYE YOU CAN FIND
A RARE SPECIES OF HERRING CALLED
TWAITE SHAD, WHICH IS ONLY FOUND
IN FOUR RIVERS IN THE UK.

Welsh kept intervening anyway. My grasp of the actual words and what they stood for was almost non-existent.

Tudor was all over me. "You're still putting a double u in "gwlad".

I was sure I was. I liked the "enn wog eon o vree" bit, it made some sort of muscular vocal sense. But there never seemed to be enough room for all the tongue and palette manoeuvres that the surprisingly short third sentence required.

I am sure Welsh is not a challenging language to learn. Nor is Chinese. But Chinese is rendered into the most simple of Latin phonetics. "Dong fang hung, tai yang shen," goes the Chinese National anthem – especially if sung by Winston Churchill. It's not very close to the correct Cantonese inflection or pronunciation. Some even consider it slightly racist. But you get by. An entire coach of mainland Chinese once joined with my rendition of "The East is Red" on a motorway running through Hong Kong. Not many Welshmen would have done the same in Tintern as I trudged across that hayfield. I later discovered that my rural idyll had ruined the hay even more than the song.

Meanwhile, Brian, our sound recordist, was urging me on. He sang his version, which, to my ears, might as well have been "The East is Red". It got him by at rugby matches, he told me, and he went to a lot of them. I tried listening to him. That really mucked me up. Now I had a sort of pidgin version of the great classic rattling in my brain.

Just over the bridge and halfway into the village of Tintern I ran across an impressive little secondhand bookshop, perhaps an overspill from Hay-on-Wye, now only a few miles upriver.

It specialised in children's books, and amongst the mint edition Rupert Bear annuals I found a leather-bound collection of early ballads. But the title page informed me that the book in my hands was printed in the very early years of the nineteenth century. No Welsh National Anthem even existed then.

"Hen Wlad Fy Nhadau" was written in 1856 by a father and son team, the James gang, (Evan and James James). It was written as a dance tune. James junior was that Welsh musical hero, a harpist, who played in the local pub. His song, "The Banks of the Rhondda" was composed in Pontypridd (home to my Aunty Betty, though she seldom danced). It had a six-eight time signature. It became increasingly popular as a jig, so much so that it began to be sung at sporting events, to warm up the crowd.

Wales actually gave the tradition of singing the anthem before a rugby game to the world when, in 1905, it was decided to sing the anthem to compete with the All Blacks' Haka. But of course crowds can't dance, they can only wallow and so the tune gradually slowed and grew in portentousness until it took on the rousing form that it enjoys today. Thank goodness for that. Had it had been any faster I would have been slower getting hold of it. All that remained after all the ministrations I had received were a few scraps of paper and a distant memory of the tune.

I needed help and I found it in the form of Ruth Sweet. Ruth offered the musical support that I needed. She picked me up and swept me westwards to Rhaglan. She said her handbell ringing group would accompany me. Now, for the first time, I was seriously cruising into the soothing green of Monmouthsire, and with my stuff in a Range Rover boot, to boot.

"My father always used to say that this was God's own country," Ruth told me, as we swooped between the neat hedges. "I worked as a teacher and my husband, who is in computers, had postings in southern Ireland and Florida. But as we came to retirement, you know, I had to come back." She waved a hand in the direction of the misty ridge ahead. "You can see why."

"And are those the Black Mountains?" I asked, naming Welsh mountain ranges randomly.

"No, they are much further away. What we can see are the lower parts of the Brecon Beacons. That's the Sugar Loaf Mountain over there. Abergavenny is just beyond it."

Coming from Essex, I loved this vision of "over the hills and far away". Welsh vistas always provided a valley to drop into, a plain to cross or mountains to climb. In Essex the horizon tended to be flat, even and built over.

The handbells had been discovered in a trunk in St Cadoc's Church in Rhaglan, while the place was being decorated with flowers for a festival. There were two octaves of single bells on leather strap handles, many of which had worn away with age. Later it was established that they had been made in London near King's Cross and, since the foundry had ceased to exist in 1852, they could certainly be declared "old".

The group decided to have the bells restored as a millennium project and then learned to play them. They took the name "The St Cadoc's Millennium Chimes" and their very first performance was given by candlelight, because of a power cut. Since then they have taken on some experienced hand-ringing assistance and learned to play from notation. So this is what I was confronted with now – a score.

We ate "cawl", the Welsh soup of vegetables and lamb, and then we went through into Ruth's front room. A large book was dumped in front of me and two bells were placed in my hands.

"You swing forward following the shape of a rugby ball," I was told firmly. "You swing it out with a smooth movement. Flick... and back."

I didn't want to say that it was a long time since I had handled a rugby ball. But I got the general idea: another accomplishment that I could perform, if I acted the part. I just had to pretend to be a handbell ringer and no doubt I would become one. I had to embrace the team spirit too. Despite all the beautifully made-up eyes watching me I was after all just two notes in a musical instrument.

I extended my arm and swayed into it a bit, like a child overcome with music in the infants' choir, and a sonorous "dong" rang around Ruth's front room. Everybody applauded. Fair enough.

Now all sixteen of us bent to our task. Reading the score was surely going to be more complex, but, luckily, it was a matter of "beats". I was responsible for two notes. Each was clearly marked in dayglo colours on my sheet. As long as I could get with the rhythm and extend my arm on cue I would probably contribute. And with fifteen other experienced ringers to help I was in a good place. After all, I only had a choice of two notes. I just had to remember my right from my left. Mostly, I managed.

Let me just say that, in the close confines of a suburban home in Rhaglan, a double octave of bells played by sixteen dedicated players can deliver a wondrous clamour of music. The bells rang out in clear, resonant notes and the vocals rumbled along somewhere in amongst them. Whether a slight residue of double "u"s, wrongly accented double "dd"s, false "th"s instead of "dd"s, "f"s for "v"s, or "yous" insteads of "ayes" emerged, I must leave to others to judge. (Preferably not Welsh speakers).

Let's just say that Brian, our sound engineer, was satisfied that my version would have been "OK on the terraces of the Millennium Stadium". For my part, I was satisfied that Brian was an expert sound recordist and a fine judge of singing. And you will be satisfied he knew how to bury a dismal cacophony of pseudo-Welsh gibberish deep in the tuneful harmony of some expertly jangled handbells.

It was the anthem. And lovely music too. We should be grateful for that.

I was. Deeply. But I was no nearer the mysteries of one of the most important and rightly revered bastions of Welsh culture, the language. It and I remain on the shelf. It will have to come, but later, later, later.

# – 2 –
# BEACONS
## INTO THE GREEN

COUNT
BELISARIUS
ROBERT GRAVES

THE SILENCE
OF COLONEL
BRAMBLE
ANDRÉ MAUROIS

John Macnab
JOHN BUCHAN

MR WESTON'S
GOOD WINE
T. F. POWYS

THE SAILOR'S
RETURN &
BEANY-EYE
DAVID
GARNETT

THE GUN
C. S. FORESTER

THE VIRG
THE O

he Evidence
of Love

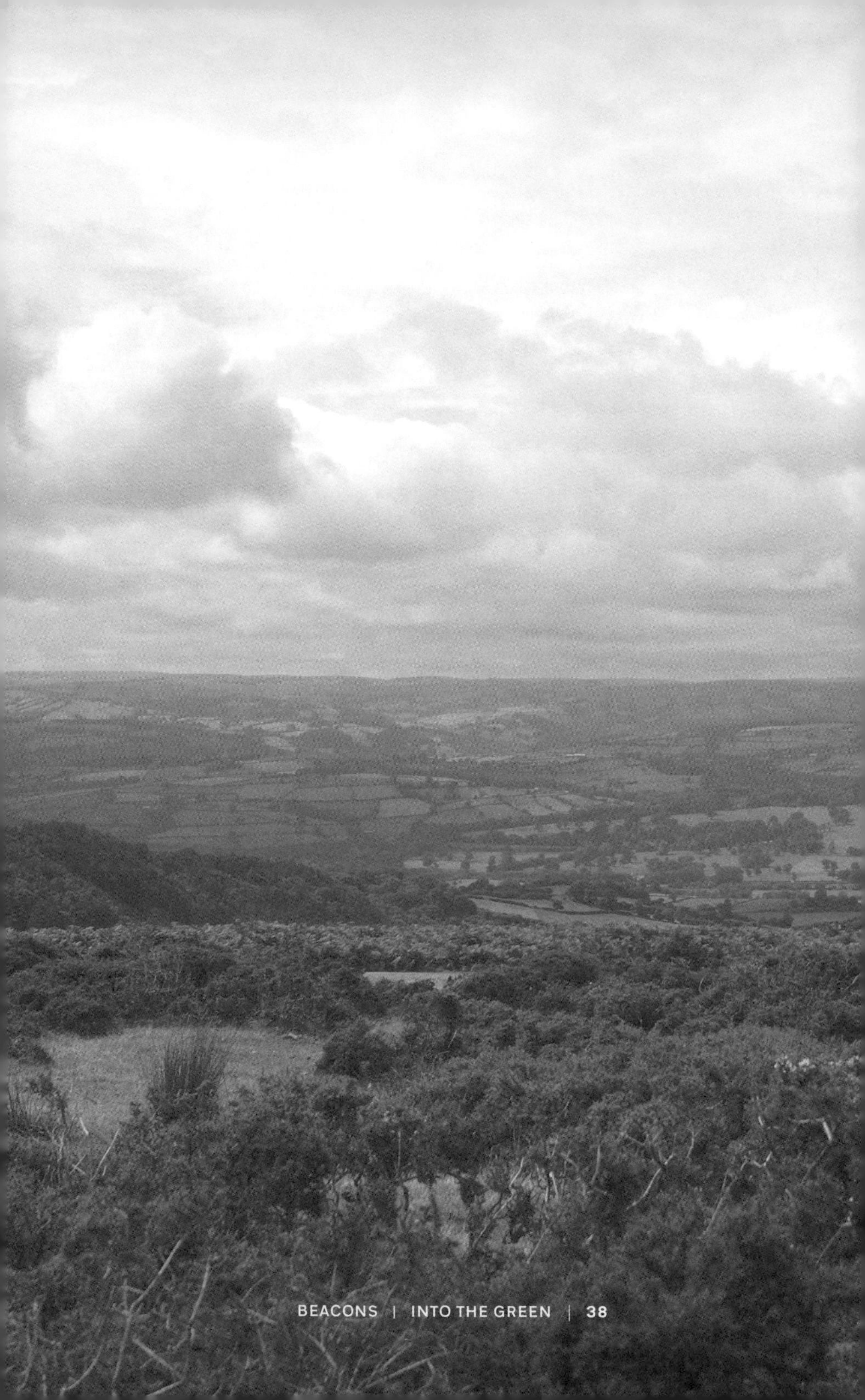

# – HAYWIRE·ON·WYE –

I think Chris, our director, hoped that the market opposite the hotel on
the square in the middle of Hay would gradually take on the appearance
of a Breughel-like, medieval fete. (Perhaps it will on film.) It felt like a
miserable collection of bric-a-brac stalls to me.

"Just come towards the camera," he called.

I had to totter through a handsome Georgian door and then
stroll nonchalantly across the road towards the bustling market folk,
spouting platitudes.

The first take was abandoned. A 50 foot tour bus stopped in front
of me and brake-farted. The second take was drowned by a motorbike.
The third and fourth got me skipping around speeding BMWs. The
final attempt was interrupted by an elderly Australian who wanted my
autograph. I don't mind Australians. They are a temporary nuisance. It's
the traffic that gets me. Every town I visit would work better if they just
shut the bloody place to all the bloody cars.

Other than that, Hay is, of course, a big success. It is a "book
town". It is said that there are more books per head in Hay than in
any other town in the world. I first went there twenty-five years ago to
interview the self-styled "King" of Hay, Richard Booth, for a series called
"The Bookworm".

He told me that he was indifferent to books. (He was teasing me,
and the producer, particularly, who started to sweat.) But of course he
loves books; it is said that Richard Booth himself has two million books,
equating to 10 miles of bookshelves. His battle, however, he explained,
was not for books but for the soul of Hay. In the seventies, Hay's High
Street was dominated by unoccupied, rotting shops. Richard was an
early campaigner against bypass megastores. He was one of the first to
finger Tesco as the great Satan, the massive Moloch, the Miltonic lord of
expensive sacrifice. He needed something to keep the town alive and he
hit on dead books.

"It could have been almost anything," he explained. "I don't
think of Hay as a book town, I think of it as a single commodity town.
I reasoned that if all the old books were gathered in one place then
collectors would come."

I bought into Richard's big plan. I visualised other towns becoming "diving equipment towns", or "secondhand art towns", or "model motorcar towns". Even then, in the late eighties, Richard could point to two copycat book burghs in the US, and another one in France.

But I didn't buy a book. I wandered off into his buckram-covered world in a stupor. Every shop had a damp cardboard smell. Long shelves bent under the burden of slightly-foxed Everyman editions and faded encyclopedias. It looked like home. Faced with such a bewildering choice and no pressing need, I couldn't make up my mind: the complete plays of J.B. Priestley, an out-of-date restaurant guide to Rome, a ten-year-old history of a Balkan campaign in the Second World War? There was no end to the publications I didn't really need, so I didn't choose. In a town of a million cheap secondhand books I bought nothing at all. Not even a Simenon for the train back.

My challenge was to swim in a mountain lake. So I was planning to leave the town for the hills in search of something wet and freezing. I even had a joke. "I would never be able to buy a swimming costume in a book town, eh?"

But now I was back in Hay, I noticed that it was no longer exclusively a book town at all.

There were antique shops, knick-knack shops, perfumed candle shops, antique Welsh blanket shops and humid cafés, but, in order to make my laboured point on camera, we had to actively search for bookshops. We found the detective and thriller centre, the poetry bookshop and countless racks up near the castle, but Hay had turned into "a destination town". And I had to find another destination up a hill and swim in it to prove my Welsh hardiness.

Tempted by the wholly unsuitable five-toed, acid-green rubber shoes in the window, I found what I think Richard Booth had wanted to preserve all along: a straightforward, up-and-down, old-fashioned haberdashers on the main square. The autumn rain was pattering against the door. The season for wild swimmers was over. They usually stocked bathing suits, but nothing remained in my size. So I discussed the likelihood of extreme weather with the son of the proprietor. "In the Beacons," he told me, "extreme weather is not extreme. It is normative."

I pondered this and bought a massive navy-blue coverall waterproof poncho in its own carry bag.

We would have left Hay immediately, but we had an invitation to a regal event. Richard Booth had been the victim of a stroke, but it happened to be his birthday. There was a lunchtime celebration in a club down by the church. We arrived early. While I ate an organic lamb burger I watched the King of Hay's courtiers roll in, sporting the tatterdemalion flourishes of a once flourishing middle-class hippy set. A pug ran around yapping at ankles. Wine glasses were raised and filled and filled again. A man in a black suit on a balcony sang the Hay National Anthem.

Richard, with a gleam in his eye, joined me on a sofa. He outlined his new campaign, bursting with the old rebel mettle. The mantra had changed. Hay was no longer solely a book town. It was a "tourist" town too. (As indeed it was.) It provided jobs and supported a population of roughly 1500. The Hay Festival brings in over 80,000 writers, publishers and literature fans. Bill Clinton dubbed the festival "The Woodstock of the Mind". But something was amiss.

I gradually gathered that the Welsh Assembly Government and Sky Television had made an unholy pact to seize the Hay-on-Wye Book Festival. This was to be resisted. Rupert and James were mentioned in unflattering terms. The centralising effect of the Welsh Assembly was disparaged.

I wanted to dig deeper, but Richard was ushered outside, to sit under his flags of office, wearing a tin crusader helmet, surrounded by adoring women in cotton print dresses. Toasts were offered. New vows of eternal resistance were sworn. It reminded me of *Passport to Pimlico*. Perhaps it was a fanciful idea. Maybe it was parochial. Except that those few book towns that we had discussed, nearly thirty years before, had now grown to number two hundred, worldwide. There are "food towns" too, in Ludlow and Abergavenny. I still fantasise that there might one day be an "old paintings town".

While governments fret uselessly about the high street, Hay is packed. And Richard Booth has proved conclusively that local commitment can make the difference.

In the meantime I had hired a bright red Vespa scooter and mounted up to drive out into the Beacons and link cool, cosmopolitan Hay with rugged, out-there Brecon.

Like other iconic vehicles, the Vespa was conceived in the ashes of WWII. Similar to the Lambretta, the Vespa was inspired by an American military scooter called the Cushman, which was used by the Americans to circumnavigate the German lines while fighting on the borders of Italy. This, however, was not Italy. It was Wales and it had started raining.

# HAY FACTS

THE TOWN OF HAY-ON-WYE IS TWINNED
WITH TIMBUKTU IN MALI.

---

THE HAY FESTIVAL BRINGS OVER 80,000
WRITERS, PUBLISHERS AND LITERATURE
FANS FROM AROUND THE WORLD. HALF
OF THE FESTIVAL'S AUDIENCE COMES
FROM WALES, WITH OVER 225,000 TICKETS
BEING SOLD FOR THE 2012 EVENT.

---

ON 1 APRIL 1977, RICHARD BOOTH
(WHO IS RESPONSIBLE FOR HAY'S
TRANSFORMATION) PROCLAIMED HAY AN
INDEPENDENT KINGDOM AND HE WAS CROWNED
KING AND RULER OF THE NEW STATE. HIS HORSE
WAS NAMED PRIME MINISTER.

---

AS PART OF THIS APRIL FOOLS JOKE,
MR BOOTH DEVISED A NATIONAL ANTHEM,
GAVE OUT NATIONAL PASSPORTS AND
CREATED AN EDIBLE CURRENCY OUT
OF RICE PAPER.

---

THERE ARE MORE BOOKS PER HEAD IN HAY
THAN IN ANY OTHER TOWN IN THE WORLD.

# – WELSH WATER –

I have never really wanted to quench my thirst from a babbling brook. What about that decomposing sheep up the glen, the fertiliser in the punctured plastic sack, or the cow hormones in those incontinent cows at the water hole? And yet I regularly drink gallons of refrigerated mineral water, advertised as gushing out of some mountain spring. I needed guidance.

The water for Brecon Carreg comes in from a couple of nondescript huts in the undergrowth round the back of the bottling factory. "No, I can't show you where our source is." Jeff, our helper, was emphatic. "It's a security issue."

I nodded, unsure whether he thought we might steal it, or return in the middle of the night to poison it, but now I was confused. I had been told that we were going to the source. In fact I was getting "source" mixed up with "*le source*" thanks to my source (in the information sense). I hope you're following this.

I finally gathered that we were planning to get a look at a river in a cave somewhere else much later on. Nonetheless my confusion served to confuse the director and Jeff, and my information source for a good half an hour, until Jeff took me to a laboratory where a computer could show me the true origin of his own water.

Brecon Carreg water comes from wells and not from a babbling stream at all. Unlike the famous Perrier "*source*" (which is French for spring) there was no unending spout of fizzing "*eau*". The well-heads were undistinguished boxes sitting in the bushes round the back of the factory. The water may be called "spring" water. It was supine water in reality.

Nonetheless, the computer was reassuring. It showed three bright blue vertical bars. Each represented the level in one of Jeff's wells. For some reason the company never seemed to bother with one of them. "You can ignore that one," Jeff told me. So I did, and I stared meaningfully at the two other unwavering computer representations.

Numbers were flickering slightly. They told Jeff that he was currently extracting six or so thousand litres an hour. He could go as high as fifteen thousand litres an hour if he were filling litre bottles, but he wasn't today, so they remained steady, consistent and well within his limits.

Jeff's wells never ran dry. As furiously as Jeff extracted the water, so it seeped back from the surrounding aquifer. I was unsure why there was a limit to his powers of extraction, but there clearly was. His licence restricted him. If there was a sudden thirst for Welsh water, however, he could turn to that other well. Or even the one I had been ordered to ignore.

I liked the factory: a glittering city of stainless steel pipes and mini conveyor belts. We marvelled at the ingenuity of factory engineers for a moment or two. Machines jiggled and squirted. A magnificent, Soda-Stream contraption, which added bubbles as necessary, was, alas, idle. They were making or, rather, bottling "still" water today. So the water hurried straight to a Perspex-faced box the size of a caravan. An endless row of plastic bottles entered at one end, met a water pipe and were then combined, at bewildering speed, to create a nose-to-tail traffic jam of bottled water, which made a dainty journey along a wide sweep of conveyor to the next machine. This rotated each bottle through a label applicator and trundled the finished product to wrapping and packing to become big, heavy square blocks of compartmentalised water.

It wasn't always this formalised and industrial. Brecon Carreg (taking its name from Carreg Cennen Castle) began life as a true cottage industry in 1978, but with the help of big investors had taken on mythical overtones. Unadorned nature was meeting highly complex, chemical artificiality. We were all dressed in robes and blue hair nets, which stole our identity and transformed us into sinister robot figures. "We can follow the conveyor belt along to make it look funny," I told Tudor.

"There's nothing funny about this." said a passing humanoid in a hairnet, firmly.

Jeff explained that they provided several different varieties of bottled water. The most complex was their mineral water. "You cannot call any old water 'mineral water'," he said. " 'Mineral water' has to be monitored for two years to check its consistency."

"So what minerals do you have in your mineral water?" I asked Jeff, innocently.

He hesitated.

"It's all on the label," he said.

I had a look. The water was low in sodium at 5mg per litre. But there were 55mg of calcium and some silica, sulphate, magnesium, potassium and nitrate. It was all utterly meaningless to me. I am sure other shoppers examine it minutely.

Later, however, when I finally got to see a river emerging from the cave, several miles from the factory, I began to understand the science of it all. My guide was Gary, a caving enthusiast. He explained that the southwestern extremities of the Brecon Beacons are "Karst Country": a geologist's term for a limestone landscape.

Limestone is created by the skeletons of sea creatures, deposited on an ancient seabed hundreds of millions of years ago. They died so we could cave and sup clean water. The movement of the earth's crust crushed this stuff into layers of rock. It was laid down in an ocean in the Tropics and made its way to Wales by creaking and juddering across the surface of the planet.

Limestone is eroded by water but in a gratifyingly slow manner. (Everything in geology takes ages – especially the explanations.) Water and lime together create a light carbonic acid. This eats holes into the solid rock: potholes if they are vertical and caves if they are horizontal. Cavers like Gary thrust themselves bodily through fissures and cracks in the stone in order to explore these holes and discover and enjoy (in their own fashion) many kilometres of passages and voids hung with lengthy icicles of rock (which have also taken an inconceivably long time to form). Water just drips through.

The Beacons are a caving hotspot. The Dan yr Ogof cave system is said to be the largest in Europe and covers some 11 miles. Many of these caves have yet to be explored. Experts argue there could be as much as a 100 miles of tunnel. Porth yr Ogof cave meanwhile (also in the Beacons) has one of the largest cave entrances in the United Kingdom. It is 20 metres wide and 3 metres high.

As we stood looking at the stream pouring out of the low cliff, Gary told me that I was right to "avoid surface water". He confirmed my prejudices. "A lot of unhealthy things can float on the surface of stagnant water," he explained. He pointed instead to the gushing river below us. "This stuff has been through eight kilometres of cleansing rock. It is perfectly safe to drink."

Any water that is not following crevices and emerging in torrents after an 8-kilometre underground journey is steadily seeping downwards through the rock. This is even safer. The limestone acts as an extended natural filter.

"It takes around fifteen years from the point where it falls on the hillside to the time it enters our wells," Jeff told me back at the factory. This is the long period of filtration and cleansing. This is when the minerals come. This is why they bottle it."

So now we drank the stuff: the mineral water first. I spat and gobbled and swilled, but I felt as if I was cleaning my teeth, so I drank it instead. It tasted entirely neutral. Some mineral waters, especially French ones, are so soapy I avoid them. This was bland. So was the other water, the "spring water", which was, effectively, as far as I could tell, the same water with a different name. It came from a well, not a spring at all, but the arcane food and drink legislation allowed it to be labelled incorrectly.

"We have applied for that well to be classified as 'mineral water' too," Jeff told me.

I wasn't sure why. To my ears 'spring' sounds rather more refreshing than a 'mineral'. Of course, they knew that already. That's why they used the word.

So why bother with the 'mineral' designation at all? Are there that many British hypochondriacs sharing a European belief in the liver-cleansing properties of almost undrinkable, carbonic-flavoured waters? I discovered, however, that Brecon Carreg was now owned by Belgians. No doubt these hypochondriac continentals wanted the certification. Perhaps they were unaware that the British increasingly prefer water with added chemical "strawberry" or "lemon" flavour, manufactured in laboratories in the mid-west of America, and with plenty of extra sugar to ensure that the healthy properties of pure water are utterly extinguished.

Bottled water is ironic in the Beacons, which has 17 reservoirs in its hills. The water that flows through the plumbing is, surely, effectively the same as the bottled product that this Belgian company delivers by road. Tasted much the same to me too. It tasted like water, in fact.

"Do you have any of that fizzy stuff?" I asked Jeff.

"Oh yes," he said. "The machine is off today but we certainly make it," and he offered me some to try.

This was much better. Instead of bland, still, tasteless, ordinary water, I had a mouthful of bubbles. Please, don't morally legislate against my last remaining vice. You have your beer and Coke. I just want to drink carbonised water. The only thing I object to is its name. The description "sparkling water" was made up by a canny marketing executive. Yes, I know – like diamonds glittering in a fairy's diadem, it "sparkles" and "twinkles", but it is carbon dioxide pumped in under pressure. "Carbon dioxide water" might not sell. "Fizzy water" sounds juvenile. At least when you get to Belgium they comprehend "with gas".

I asked Jeff what distinguished his water. He plunged in. "Refreshing… low on sodium… clean…," but he was faltering. Then inspiration hit him. "… Welsh!" He said finally with a note of triumph in his voice.

I drank to that.

# – UP IN THE AIR –

In Llangernyw I met a chimney sweep and accused him of coming from Liverpool. He looked pained and told me he was sixth generation Colwyn Bay and fully Welsh-speaking. (The coast in the far north has a very distinct accent. There are high "ees" in it.)

He also explained that down in the Valleys the recognisable Welsh lilt returned. Not recognisable enough for me to identify another woman I met in Pembrokeshire, who had been born in Cardigan, raised in Birmingham and now lived in Haverfordwest. It was better not to try to guess at origins, but Bo was clearly not Welsh.

"I was born in Sweden," he explained, "but I lived for a long time in New Zealand. I still live there in the summer." (I think he might have meant our winter.) But the much travelled Bo, who later explained that he had worked as a seaman for many years in his youth and had used the skills, he'd learned in ice-breaking runs through the Gulf of Finland to open a restaurant near Wellington, had chosen to come to the Beacons.

I run into these people from time to time. The Finns with a hotel in Fishguard. The girls who ran away from Amsterdam to west Wales. When fervent Welsh apologists get bitter about helicopter shots of their landscape and want informed opinion to concentrate on Welsh achievement (heavy industry and its after-affects mainly) they are missing a point. Wales is incredibly beautiful. Rural Wales was a life-changing revelation for this exile, previously familiar only with Cardiff and Newport.

Admittedly, I was fortunate. I travelled for six weeks and hit perhaps three days of rain. The day I met Bo was one of the wet days. We stood in the hangar by the Black Mountains Gliding Club airfield, a meadow raised up on the side of a mountain, like a landing strip in the Alps, and gazed at the de-tumescent orange windsock through a light drizzle.

The gliders lay jumbled around us. Their crucifix forms required a criss-cross parking method. What frail and insubstantial kites they seemed in the frigid top-light of the roof. Single-handed gliders looked little stronger than the dubbing-daubed, tissue paper balsa-wood models I made when I was twelve. Those had required hours of patient work with ball-topped pins and sweet intoxicant glue, and usually crashed and smashed to splinters on their first flight.

Bo stood by a dual-seater glider. It looked a bit stronger than my kits, but clearly the lack of any means of propulsion permitted a return to utter basics. The hull clasped its two riders in a tight embrace. There was a long wing and bit of tube for a fuselage. But we weren't going up today.

"The rain reduces visibility too much," Bo explained. "And we need thermals, rising air caused by variations in temperature, to get us flying. This is not the weather for that."

So we waited. He told me how he worked here as an instructor. Bo had chosen the area because this was the best place to glide in Britain. The average flight times were the longest in the UK. The lie of the land provided rising air and challenging flying, but the landscape was spectacular. He didn't need my prompting. Bo loved the Beacons. He was daily astonished by the landscape laid out beneath him.

We left. We couldn't go that day, though, even in that rain, the hills were garlanded with smoke-like headdresses of mist and the dark clouds softened the greens to a flat, fuzzy brilliance.

When we came back the following afternoon the sock was full and the sun was shining. I was introduced to the saggy bag of cloth that was my parachute and Bo took me through the drills necessary to get me airborne. "The biggest danger is the idea of hitting another plane," he said. "Just pull open the hood, unclip your safety belt and jump clear and then reach down and pull this metal ring and the parachute will open."

This was five more things than I would be capable of doing if I was hurtling to the ground to my death, but it was notable how focused I was on these instructions, compared with the ones that drone out on EasyJet.

"Look down at the ring," Bo continued. "It will give you something to concentrate on and you will get it." He was talking now as if some mid air collision was a pre-ordained part of our jaunt. "Otherwise you could pull the harness off." Well, we didn't want to do that, did we?

He sat me in the front: great views through a plastic hood. He went through his instrument check-list aloud. Someone tied a rope to a hook below us and the two of us, together in a cabin smaller than the average dodgem car, were attached to a former crop-spraying plane, which whirred and bumped off across the vivid lawn, dragging us behind it.

"We're up now," Bo said, seconds later. The tow-plane wasn't. For a while we flew at no more than 10 feet off the ground, but, before the hill sloped away to the village below, the plane got up into the air, banked a little and began to climb upwards.

Our tow seemed further away than I had imagined it would be. Our rope bent a little under its own weight, stretching out to this airborne workhorse, dragging us up. And then further up.

"I will need you to keep an eye open for other aircraft," Bo told me. I kept both eyes open. Suddenly, with a slight jerk the rope was gone, and there was a falling feeling in my stomach. We slowed and wallowed slightly as if walking now, without a hand to hold us.

Now, apart from the rushing air, we were noiselessly suspended like an albatross. We were circling above a valley, picked out in a cold, yellow, slanting September light. There were clouds but they were high. A relief map of the National Park was laid out around us.

"There's the Wye Valley," Bo said indicating the river slipping though trees and fields. "That's an Iron-Age hill fort there to the left."

The sun caught the outlines of the faded earthworks on the grey top of a hill, which like the others, like the Beacons themselves, rose bare and bun-shaped out of richer, greener, valleys.

The Brecon Beacons cover 500-odd square miles and we could probably see them all. There are 30 standing stones within the boundaries of the National Park and over a thousand separate farms, divided restlessly by hedges into rectangular forms following the contours of the valleys. It was a majestic artwork that had taken thousands of years to create.

I was entranced by the dead-end valleys: fingers of bottle green that crept up towards the shorn, sage hills and often ended with a high grey stone farmstead crouched down in the crack of the mountain.

The railway had had the most severely negative impact on the agricultural industry of Brecon. In 1868 there were 11,000 acres used for wheat farming. By 1930 it was down to 595. The Brecon and Merthyr Tydfil Junction Railway also had one of the country's steepest gradients, which required two to three engines to pull the train. The gradient led to runaway trains with the line being nicknamed 'Breakneck and Murder'.

Otherwise, this was a landscape that had evolved within the limits of man's once-restricted capabilities. We soared over yeoman farms, open fields for stock, and the patterns of the dispersed farm life. There was a settlement of steep-eaved buildings that I guessed was a monastery, but turned out to be a mental asylum.

Nothing about these few square miles threatened any form of future. In fact the distant future will surely look back on us and thank us for preserving them. We already look back with gratitude on the foresight of the creators of the National Parks. There are ruined, desecrated landscapes enough in Britain. But developers and their Welsh Assembly Government allies don't want to expend energy trying to remake these bad suburbs and hopelessly designed, alienating places. They want to suck on the indefinable high that we feel in this carefully made landscape, by

# BRECON BEACONS FACTS

THE BRECON BEACONS NATIONAL PARK IS
520 SQUARE MILES AND HAS A POPULATION
OF AROUND 30,000.

PEN Y FAN IS THE HIGHEST POINT IN SOUTHERN
BRITAIN, STANDING AT 886M.

MAEN LLIA IS SAID TO BE THE HIGHEST STANDING
STONE IN SOUTH WALES AT AN ALTITUDE OF 573M.

GEORGE EVEREST, THE MAN WHO MOUNT EVEREST
IS NAMED AFTER WAS BORN IN CRICKHOWELL
IN THE BRECON BEACONS.

NORTH OF BRECON YOU'LL FIND LLANWRTYD WELLS,
THE SMALLEST TOWN IN BRITAIN,
WHICH IS ALSO HOME TO THE WORLD BOG
SNORKELLING CHAMPIONSHIPS.

ONE OF THE SMALLEST DISTILLERIES IN THE WORLD,
PENDERYN, IS IN THE FOOTHILLS OF THE
BRECON BEACONS.

THE VILLAGE OF LLANFRYNACH, SOUTH OF BRECON,
WAS HOME TO ONE OF THE WEALTHIEST
ROMAN CIVILIAN ESTABLISHMENTS KNOWN
IN CENTRAL AND NORTHERN WALES.

DR WILLIAM AUBREY, ONE OF THE FOUNDERS
OF JESUS COLLEGE OXFORD, WAS BORN
IN BRECKNOCKSHIRE.

WHEN THE BRECON AND MERTHYR RAILWAY FIRST
OPENED IT HAD THE HIGHEST TUNNEL IN THE
COUNTRY AT 1313FT ABOVE SEA LEVEL.

building more here. They know its marketable value. They want to destroy its very success by offering it to the estate agent. So, away with green belt – let's colonise more of the beautiful places.

A few days before Bo and I soared up to look at this impeccable vista, the Planning Minister Nick Boles had been floating a theory that National Parks were "kept in aspic".

"We are suffering a slight dip in our relentless material "growth", called a recession, so now we need to declare an emergency and desecrate more of our country," I shouted at Bo. "We have no policies to recycle houses like we insist on recycling paper. Our tax system encourages new building. And in the meantime it is conservationists who are accused of selfishness."

For ten minutes I disturbed the still air above the Beacons, and probably Bo, by ranting to him about the horrors of politically motivated urban sprawl.

But we were due back. In this area glides of five hours are common. We had been up for half an hour. After a few minutes more, we bumped and rutted our way onto the ground and landed without splitting into a thousand pieces of balsa.

## – AT SWIM ONE BIRD –

Llyn Cwm Llwch is a dark puddle of cobalt at the bottom of a carved bowl.

Up on the rim of the surrounding mountains, where the two flat-iron peaks of Corn Du and Pen y Fan outstare each other, I could make out minute bifurcated dots. They were ramblers walking on the very lip of the ridge, trudging up to the highest peaks in the Beacons. They gave us the scale: immense, going on gigantic. We were lucky to see the tops, apparently. Today they were unshrouded, clear, against the grey blotting-paper sky. Not much marred their flanks. No trees, some smears of shale-fall. From our distant outpost, the hills were smoothed and rounded, polished and raw.

Far below, on the shores of the lake, down in the valley, were more dots, this time sheep. I realised there were wild horses too. The Welsh mountain pony nearly fell into extinction in the sixteenth century, when King Henry VIII ordered the destruction of all stallions under 15 hands. These ones clearly found us mildly disturbing - irritating. It was not fear. Like beach-walkers, they simply did not want to be socially associated with us.

As we clambered down, so they wandered quietly upwards on the far side of the valley. As we left, I looked back. They had stationed themselves on the far northern pinnacle, waiting for us to leave.

I was glad to see them, of course, because it gave me a chance to spout my Julius Caesar fact. (He had thought them brave chariot steeds and had taken some back to Rome, though I assume he killed their riders.)

But I was here to swim. The path down to the lake was a gutter of mud. I had no fear of the tarn. I didn't think it would freeze my bollocks off. It would be cold. But I have been in the Tay in Perth in November. And just last year, while walking in the Scottish Highlands I plunged about in a mountain stream. I was keen. I just wanted to get on with it. I was oddly glad that I was going to be the only one doing it too. The others would stare at me from within their four layers of clothing, including polypropylene outer shells and waterproof Gore-Tex, like space men watching a poor bare forked animal skipping about.

Ah, yes, that was a small problem. I didn't have a swimming costume and I would be naked. What sort of exhibitionist was I, then? I liked the fact that it was raining, because it meant that the air temperature and the water temperature would feel similar, and as soon as I threw off my own fleeces and T-shirts I would be in some sort of pact with the weather and the wet. It would feel much colder to enter this water on a hot day.

So I faced the camera and remembered how Roger Deakin, the author of *Waterlog*, the original book on wild swimming, wrote about his dip in a Welsh tarn. It was his induction to the act of swimming his way across Britain.

I also recalled an evening in Diss last year when his friend Ronald Blythe, in his comfy jersey and woolly shirt, chuckled at the memory of Roger plunging into every available waterhole he passed. Yup, he recognised the determined egotism of the act; the same egotism that I was now enjoying.

And then there was Alan Clarke, the politician. He wrote about stopping in his Riley or Allard or Supercharged Bentley, or some other out-of-date car, by a Scottish lake and taking a dip, which, he said, felt as invigorating as cocaine. Though why this friend of Mrs Thatcher and one-time cabinet minister should know what cocaine felt like, one can only speculate.

It was nothing like cocaine. There was the usual slippery entrance stumble, and though the rocks were blessedly flat they were smeared with gooey sediment, the sort of shitty sensation that I might have once recoiled from, but I now recognised as a harmless, freshwater sludge.

The camera was rolling. Everybody else – researcher, photographer, guide, sound, camera and director – was standing behind it wrapped in protective gear.

I tried a few tentative steps and met a soft and deep spongy weed. It was possibly full of leeches. Leeches are said to gather in the "*llyn*". This might also have been slightly disturbing. In fact it was merely comfortable underfoot.

All my trepidation was banished by an assumption of rectitude. That was it. I had an aura of Leslie Stephens, that Victorian mountain pioneer, about me now. Only mortal petty-bourgeois fuddy-duddies would stand askance and trembling. This was what real men of the mountain did. It separated the wild horses from the sheep. I even reached down and casually disentangled various bits of my frontal arrangements.

Sod everybody. I dropped down into the black water. It was more soft than freezing, speckled with raindrops and wrinkled with wind. And then I struck out and swam away across the deep area, where a legendary invisible fairy island once stood. The legend says it tempted the locals. They took part in an annual Beltane feast, out in the middle of the dark waters, until one stole an apple. It turned to maggots in his hand and the door was shut on mere mortals forever.

The water, like all lake swimming water, was sweet in the mouth: no chlorine, no salt. It had a peppery, slightly silty taste. No limestone filters here. I wondered, as I splashed about and completed this "Celtic Challenge", whether this really did link me with my Welsh roots. Surely not many of my fellow countrymen, lurking in the shopping centres of the post-industrial Welsh hinterland, actually swam in wild waters?

And that's what swimming in a Welsh mountain lake did for me. An unappealling sense of my own specialness surfaced alongside my pallid dugs in the black water. I think Shelley and Alan Clarke probably felt much the same. Roger Deakin, on the other hand, was far too nice. But at least, for a moment or two, I was at one with Welsh wilderness and away with the fairies.

— 3 —

# GOWER

WILD RUGBY FOOD

# – BEACHED WALES –

If Wales is a geological "continent in miniature" with its mountains and lakes, populous sea ports and a vast unending steppe (except that last bit, of course, unless you include parts of Borth), then the Gower is a continent in miniature, in miniature: a jut of land that reaches out in the north of the Bristol Channel towards the Atlantic Ocean between Swansea and Llanelli. It seems to cram the lot into its 15 mile length.

Gower is not especially rugged, except on a few cliff tops, although almost a third of it is a nature reserve. It is comfortable and reassuring. It has deep woods, and sunken lanes with high beech canopies. It has foggy marshes, stony coves and high wild moorland. It has untroubled farmland, hidden meadows, long wild strands and bleak outcrops. Just about the only things it lacks are a geyser and a grizzly bear problem. And all this just a short bus ride from Swansea.

The bus is vital. There is no train station in the Gower. In the nineteenth century the Lord of Margam thought 'the rail would destroy the country'. His order not to build a railway has been followed to this day. In 1956 the Gower became the first area in Britain to be designated an Area of Outstanding National Beauty.

So I started in Swansea, which I love. I know it well and I feel entitlement. I used to own it – if only in Russell T Davies's imagination. In the early part of the century he wrote a drama series for ITV called "Mine All Mine" and I played a taxi driver who, thanks to an ancient title deed, found that he had inherited the ownership of the city. We filmed everywhere, enjoying the ice cream from Joe's, the fishing from the Mumbles pier and the lascivious murals by Frank Brangwyn in the town hall (if you are invited to a "Best Welsh Sausage Award", go.) The paintings are extraordinary and were banned from the House of Lords for being 'too flamboyant'. Too many naked breasts, they meant.

I remember the grand sweep of the beach and the curry houses by the university. Russell said at the time that if "Mine All Mine" failed to take wing, then it was probably the end for modern Welsh comedy drama. Alas, it merely bounced along the landing strip, but, luckily, along came "Gavin and Stacey" and that soared into the stratosphere. Wales became cool, but not with us.

I take the blame. There was one long speech on the top of a hill in

# GOWER FACTS

WITH 257 PEOPLE PER SQUARE KILOMETRE
THE AREA IS MORE DENSELY POPULATED
THAN WALES AS A WHOLE.

---

THERE ARE 101 LISTED BUILDINGS IN THE AREA
OF OUTSTANDING NATURAL BEAUTY,
INCLUDING FOUR GRADE I BUILDINGS.

---

THERE ARE 25 SITES OF SPECIAL SCIENTIFIC
INTEREST IN THE GOWER.

---

THE GOWER HAS FOUR BLUE FLAG BEACHES:
PORT EYNON, CASWELL BAY, LANGLAND BAY
AND BRACELET BAY.

---

IN 1904, EVAN ROBERTS, A MINER
FROM LOUGHOR (LLWCHWR), JUST
OUTSIDE SWANSEA, WAS THE LEADER
OF WHAT HAS BEEN CALLED
ONE OF THE WORLD'S GREATEST
PROTESTANT RELIGIOUS REVIVALS.

---

IN ALL, OVER 700 PLANT SPECIES
HAVE BEEN RECORDED HERE.

the first episode where my Welsh accent set off on a worldwide expedition, visiting Mumbai and Northern Ireland before coming to rest in Windsor Davies – "insufficiently Welsh", I fear.

During the making of that series I lived in a cottage on the Gower. I vividly remember my five o'clock starts to get to make-up in the Mumbles, driving off, with the light creeping over the hills, to weave past wild horses and through herds of half-awake sheep. There is a type of horse unique to this area called a 'Gower pony'. It is said there are hundreds of them on the Gower common lands. Through centuries of living and breeding on rough grazing, they have become happy to eat tough plants such as brambles and gorse. And too tough to get out of the way of cars.


## – RHOSSILI –

The far end of the Gower peninsula terminates in a claw of headland with two rocky outcrops at either end of it and a huge, sweeping, knock-you-dead beach in-between. It is a favourite for sunset photographs. Somebody has worked out that Rhossili is the seventh most photographed sunset beach in the world (a jigsaw manufacturer perhaps?). You may remember it from the Opening Ceremony of the London 2012 Olympic Games when a youth choir sang "Bread of Heaven" from there and it was broadcast at the Olympic stadium. Or not.

I went out for a morning run, on a stretch of perfect sand, littered with razor shells, soft worn wood and the very occasional bit of faded polyester rope. At the back of the shore is a small crumbling earth cliff and, between the top of that and the beginning of the hill, sits a single, white-painted cottage and its stone outbuildings. It was once a rectory and was plonked down between two parishes, so that the vicar had an equal distance to walk to his Sunday businesses. Today it is available to rent from the National Trust and is possibly the most desirable British holiday cottage on earth.

I kept looking up at it as I bounced along. Already there were dog-walkers, toddlers and earnest beachcombers dotted about on the sand, and then two blokes passing a rugby ball ran on either side of me. As they did so, they passed their ball into my hands and I discovered my "challenge" inexpertly taped to it. Apparently, I was to find and cook "a feast for a rugby hero".

Surely, you ask, that wasn't a real surprise, was it? That was a set-up. You knew that that ball was coming your way. And, since you ask – of course I did. It was a contrivance. I was out, running about on this ideal beach on an ideal June morning in the name of television artifice, and if it hadn't been for the pressing needs of the cosy travelogue I would have happily run about on it for the rest of the day. Instead, I went back up to the rectory and while I was waiting for the crew to catch up I poked my nose inside. There were two ladies with pinnies in the kitchen.

"Hello," I said, " We're from the telly. I expect they've told you we were coming."

"No."

"Oh. OK."

"But come on in. We're just cleaning up for the next guests."

I didn't like to. I knew that if we filmed inside we might have to pay the National Trust. But I wasn't filming, just nosing around.

Tudor, our cameraman, whose early life seems to have been spent entirely on the very beach I had just left (or so I gathered from the amount of reminiscing he did) had recently rented these plain rooms, with the cream-painted walls and chintz curtains, to celebrate his fiftieth birthday. It was his present to himself. He had gazed on this house while building sandcastles as a kid, then while chilling around a fire as a teenager and finally chasing his own children across the sand as a grown man. But getting hold of the cottage had required the sort of foresight that only comes with a doggedly approaching significant date. Me, I never like to queue. Or book. This was my only chance to see inside the cottage.

After my inspection, to my surprise, I was told by one of the charming guardians that, for the first time she could remember, there were booking gaps later this very year.

"I imagine it must be the recession," I suggested.

She thought it might be the reputation for "unbookability" itself. People like me, believing that they couldn't ever get hold of it, were put off trying.

Tudor had another opinion. "When we took it there were broken blinds and knife handles missing." He said. "Quite honestly, the place was disappointing."

There's always a missing knife handle in paradise.

# – GIDDY UP –

I took to a horse for the next stage of my journey.

This was at a pony-trekking centre. I have done this sort of thing before. I trekked in Colorado up a mountain at a dude ranch owned by a Californian millionaire family, where I made polite conversation with what I took to be an idiot hillbilly until I discovered he was a professor of astrophysics at Berkeley. They always gave me the gentle horse. That's fine. It means you amble along in a line watching the arse ahead for several hours. In my case the arse was an accountant from New York.

Freddy, my mount in Gower, was canny enough to know that with me on board he could do what he wanted. Theoretically, I knew which bit to pull to stop him doing what he wanted. I knew I had to firmly grasp his back in my thighs. I knew that my light touch could be suddenly turned into a sharp tug. Freddy knew that too, but because I was not really competent he decided, like a twelve-year-old delinquent with a new teacher, to see how much he could provoke me.

Off we shuffled. The stables were set in a valley. We had approached it through a tree-lined drive. But as we ambled on we quickly broke through onto the uplands of the Gower and the wild moorland that runs along the top of the peninsula.

I chatted with Helen, who was riding with me. Like Ruth in the Beacons, she had been a schoolteacher and travelled the world, but had now come back to her childhood home, drawn to the beauty that now lay spread out all around her. I needed to quiz her about Llanelli. We could see it, way across the bay to the north. If I turned I could see the south shore too and knew that somewhere down there was Swansea.

Both were industrial towns. Llanelli was "tin city". Swansea was "copper metropolis" (and once home to the biggest copper smelting works in the world). Both had rugby teams that inspired passionate loyalty. Helen now supported the Scarlets. Llanelli had worn a red "first strip" since a famous game against an Irish team in 1884.

We paused. (She stopped. Freddy walked round and round in circles.) We shared memories of our early years when we gathered with our respective families around the black-and-white television to watch Rugby Internationals. Freddy fretted.

"He wants to catch up with the others," Helen explained. The rest of the pony-trekking group had gone on up the sandy track. "He's just a herd animal and he doesn't like being separated."

Llanelli Rugby Club had enjoyed huge successes in the early seventies and nineties when they had been called the "Cup Kings of Wales". The game changed to become a regional affair in 2003, but the town team had always provided top players of international quality. I would certainly be able to find a rugby hero in the area, and if not from the Scarlets then from the Whites, the original Swansea team, which was also founded in the early 1870s, and which would later come to form part of the "Ospreys" when they amalgamated with Neath. The Whites had also had huge successes in the late seventies and then again in the nineties. Twenty members of the Swansea Whites had gone on to captain Wales. Hundreds of players had been called in to the national squad. Many of them still lived in the area. I would have to ask around, but everybody would know one or two players.

Freddy was now short-stepping and turning in tight circles.

Helen told me that the Llanelli club song was "Sosban Fach". I recalled my father singing it. I think it was the only Welsh he knew. Even then it was cod-Welsh. He learned it at Welsh Internationals I expect, but it was really a Llanelli song. It meant "little saucepan" and derived from the local industry of tin-plating. Traditionally two saucepans sit on the top of Llanelli rugby posts.

Freddy was walking backwards and snorting loudly, so we couldn't talk any more. I had gone about as high as I needed. Now I wanted to get down to the coast. I dismounted, always more complicated than it might seem. A horse is much rounder than you expect. I slid off dangerously and cautiously abandoned Freddy. I would look for a rugby hero later. In the meantime I had to get down the cliffs to visit a cave.


## – CLIFFHANGER –

"Quite unnecessary," I said straight out. It was an opening gambit. First riding on a horse, now intrepid dangling from a rope. Naturally, I didn't want to throw myself off a cliff on the end of a coloured lasso at all. I was seeking a diversion, pretending that the distance we were going to drop was totally unsuitable for the television programme we were trying to make.

We were doing this abseiling sequence to add a bit of "jeopardy" to the film and, ostensibly, to get me down and onto a coastal path some 50 feet below the top of a steep, rocky cliff (typical of the southern shore of the Gower peninsula). In 1823, an ancient female skeleton was discovered not far from here, which turned out, at over 34,000 years old, to be the oldest ceremonial burial known anywhere in Western Europe. I suspect she fell off her abseiling rope.

It looked… what? About a thousand feet down? I lay cautiously peering over the edge. Other real climbers at the bottom, waiting to come up, were mere insects. But it wasn't that far really. Let's face it, they were really quite big insects and only a hundred feet below me.

I was getting crotchety though. "We don't really need to do this, do we?" I grunted.

Now, this is not properly scientific, but I believe some Welsh people can be a little "moody" at times. And when I say some "Welsh people", I mean my family. They are virtually the only Welsh people I know, so I am not working to a very large control group here. My family tend to negotiate by mood: stubbornness, panic, alarm, irritation, accusation, defensiveness or aggression. Almost anything in preference to reasoned debate. We have an armoury of emotional weapons. For my part, I sometimes manage to control myself for almost an hour at a time, but when things get tense I start instant manipulation of my immediate social surroundings.

I have abseiled before. One of the problems is that I have only ever done it on television. I can "act" abseiling, but I can't actually "do" abseiling. And now, with a proper distance to abseil, I was finding I needed to point this out.

Usually acting will do. I had just "acted" horse riding, for goodness sakes. Of course I can't ride a horse, but I've seen people doing it. I assume a straight back and supercilious air and a relaxed manner in the saddle. It's a fake.

My objection to this Gower descent was that it was too far to "act" convincingly. Having discussed the whole sequence with Chris the director, I imagined they would rope me up, and I would lower myself gingerly off a few feet of gently sloping rock. But the charming people from Dryad Bushcraft, who set up the sequence, had wanted to give the telly people their money's worth. I could see that they had tied a rope to the highest cliff in Wales, which now plunged vertically downwards for what looked like a catastrophic distance. My acting ability was about to be sorely tested by my skill set.

This was not for the first time. I once wrote holiday freebies for a daily newspaper. It was many years ago. My children were still small. In

Corsica, I needed a bit of real action and decided to take them on a "half-day canyoning expedition". What on earth made me believe that "half-day" indicated "beginner"?

The first leg involved abseiling down a waterfall, "letting go" some 15 feet above a mountain pool and plunging into the abyss below. My children stared at the prospect in terror. I stood forward. I was "dad", fearless and forthright.

"Don't worry, darlings," I said. "It's really very easy". Never having done it before, I sent my wife over the side to see how difficult it could be. She didn't break her neck, so I tried it myself. It was passable. But I got a ghastly shock when the moment came to release my hold. Mountain pools are very cold. I surfaced. Then, from the waters of a chilly mountain pool, I watched as my nine-year-old son wrestled with a French mountain guide at the top of a cliff, trying to fight off being made to do the same. Fittingly, abseiling was apparently invented by a French mountaineer called Jean Esteril Charlet in 1879. He used it to help him descend Mont Blanc. I hope he broke his neck.

I know abseiling is easy. My advice is not to argue and fret. (Being Epping Welsh, I did that anyway and fussed for the requisite ten minutes). I got myself strapped in: one belt around the middle, two smaller belts around each thigh, taking care to separate my nadgers from the buckles (the last time I forgot that little detail and descended in excruciating pain, to the lasting benefit of prime time BBC One scheduling).

I locked the various shackles into place and leaned back over the precipice. And off I went. It seems counter-intuitive. "Pretend it's easy," I told myself. I leaned back, raised my arm and the rope slithered through a metal ring, exactly as it should do, and I began to walk backwards down the cliff face.

It was easy. I even started bouncing down, whizzing the rope through the ring. And you know, since it was impossible to look down, I didn't. The slightly nervous forced smile of my helper became a mere dot above me, and I realised with a titter that I was in fact at the bottom. That wasn't so bad was it? It was over.

"Great," shouted Christopher from somewhere in the heights above me. "We're just going to bring the camera down and you can do it again."

# – CAVE BARE –

The terrible winter had had its rewards. Because of the ghastly weather, all the wild flowers had come out late, but at the same time. It was like a rock garden in Weston-super-Mare. My guide Andrew identified harebell, celandine, crocus, rock rose and an Evian mountain water bottle. Remarkably, litter is seldom a problem in these out-of-the-way areas. It would be nice to say that about the sea's edge. Most flotsam is jetsam these days: thrown away plastic rather than floating wreckage. But choughs and rock hoppers flitted about us and there was no one else to be seen.

This included the camera crew. They had gone the road-route and now Andrew and I lounged on the sharp yellow rock and watched a rescue team practising with a bright orange rib out on the surly waters beyond a great plateau of dangerous-looking stony shallows.

There was nothing "welcoming" about this coast. The incoming tide promised to cover this corrugated shelf of doom with a few feet of raging water, but I would not have liked to pilot a boat in here, which is what made the legends and stories surrounding the cove so unlikely.

Andrew took me over the edge of a jagged escarpment to peer into a cut in the rock. A sliver of sand and a slew of white, worn stone on the floor, now that the tide was out, revealed that the cove was no more than 20 feet wide and wholly exposed to the sea.

"The story is that there was a pirate family working out of this place," Andrew told me. "There is supposed to be a secret tunnel linking their house to that thing." He pointed ahead.

The end of the cove was sealed by a four-storey-high stone wall with tiny windows: like a 60-foot tall fortified house built into the cliff face.

"My own guess is that smugglers might have landed booty in the bay around the corner and brought it round here," he went on. But anyway the original purpose of the building was much more peculiar and interesting.

By now Tudor and the others had arrived, lugging the kit, so we restaged our approach to the place and finally stood looking at a tiny hole at ground level.

"Let's go in, then," Andrew said.

It wasn't immediately obvious how we did that.

He pointed to the dark hole at the bottom of the stone wall.

"We climb under there," he said. "There used to be a rope approach down the cliff, but, with the tide out, this is the easiest way," and he lay down on the pebbles and the stinking seaweed and crawled through on his belly.

I followed, heaving myself in through a gap about a foot high, and slithering upwards in the dark. "Am I now crawling over a nest of man-eating crabs?" I asked.

"No. But if I press the rock here, the cave at the back opens and a secret tunnel emerges."

There were shafts of light breaking through, somewhere high above us. The stink was bad, but it was an organic sea-stink. Beneath my feet the floor was slithery, with bladderwrack of some kind, and above our head something flapped around a bit. But there were no Indiana Jones surprises. My eyes gradually took in the back of the cave and the man-made chimney stretching above.

"It was originally built as a dovecote, sometime in the Middle Ages," Andrew said. We arched our necks and, by the dim light from the "windows", saw nest hollows high up in the structure. There were also the remains of stone stair treads on some of the outer walls.

"They came down here and took eggs and presumably pigeons," Andrew murmured.

Pigeons are rock-dwelling birds. They emigrated to cities because they found a ready source of throwaway provender and nesting holes in drainpipes and culverts that were warmer than their rocks. This strange building was somewhere at the cusp of their social evolution into the Mary Poppins nuisances that they are today. Was it quicker to use the cliff face to build this secretive bird redoubt? I suppose so. The stone was to hand and half the wall was already there. Even now, a few birds flapped in and out in the gloom high above our heads. This was a unique dovecote, but it was not going to provide me with any food for my rugby hero. I got down on my hands and knees to slither out and paused, up to my wrists in the damp black tendrils.

"What about this seaweed? Can you eat it?"

"Not that stuff," said Andrew. "There is other edible seaweed along this coast. Some of it even gets exported to Japan. But that is bladderwrack."

I could see what he meant. The stuff in my hands, amongst the jumping sand fleas, looked a little too chewy for my purposes.

# – COCKLES OF MY HEART –

Gower was full of surprises. In the north-east corner, out on the border with Llanelli, the cosy villages, hugging the lanes, gave way to a rougher cast of accommodation. The houses got greyer and more utilitarian, the streets meaner. The region became flat. This was Penclawdd, one of the largest villages on the Gower. A high sea wall ran along the road. Beyond that were the sort of saltings and swatchways I associate with Essex and a featureless English east coast shore. Gower's reassuring hills were still there, behind my back, but, ahead, a shallow strand stretched away.

We turned off the road and drove towards a big factory shed. Glyn was waiting for us with a wheezy laugh. He led me through his kingdom, into his offices to meet a welter of people, popping out of doors and shaking my hand, while he thrust a tin into the other. "This is what happens to our cockles," he said.

I looked at a flat sardine shape covered in Spanish. "We bring them ashore here, Griff, and we wash them down and then they get sent to Boston in Lincolnshire."

I was intrigued.

"It's the main distribution and cleaning centre for the UK and most of the cockles that we collect get sent to Spain. Thirty million of these cans are exported every year." Glyn had been down to Spain many times. "We can sit there in a restaurant the entire afternoon and the food and wine keep coming. But that's what the Spanish like, you see. You know tapas. Well they love cockles as tapas. They have them on the bar, like we might have crisps."

We got into his Land Rover and drove back towards the village, turning left along a rough damp road.

"You've come at the right time, because the tide is out."

His team worked a piecework rate, way out on the sands. There was little to see as we drove out there. During World War Two several gun batteries were established to both the east and west of Penclawdd. Gun-barrels were calibrated and shells were fired across the salt marsh; it was that empty. We negotiated the gullies that ran across the bay, carrying Welsh rain out to the sea, digging deep, muddy culverts in the landscape. Suddenly we were rolling and yawing down a steep incline and into thick mud, changing gears and spraying and slipping sideways though black and grey gloop.

"This used to be the old road for donkey carts, you see," Glyn went on. "My family have been digging cockles for centuries. A lot of it was done by the women in the old days." The practice of cockle picking is very much the same as it was in the past, expect now the donkeys have been replaced by all-terrain vehicles.

We were out of the mud and on to a relatively hard sand-mix, still pressing on, as if crossing a wet desert landscape and following barely discernible tracks left by other vehicles towards a few misty dots on the horizon. Cockle picking in Penclawdd dates back to Roman times.

"We take on different areas. There are places that we know." He gave a wheezy cackle. "But we mark out areas and then we move on as we exhaust them."

It was a continual rotation process. The diggers got about six hours' hard digging in before the tide came racing up the bay faster than a man could run, and now we could see them, a caravan encampment of pick-up trucks with bent figures, shovelling and scratching at the ground. There were men and women, wearing solid gumboots, well wrapped against the damp weather, and seemingly casually scattered over an acre or so.

Tommy swung himself upwards from his bent position and greeted me. I was going to have a go. So he fixed me up with gloves and handed me my equipment: a sieve and a pronged hand rake, like a bent trident on a short handle. Glyn ushered me over to a patch of mud a few yards on. He leaned down to show me. "See there, that squirting, that's them." The water lay in shallow puddles and there were tiny jets shooting up from the surface. "They are only just below the top, so they can feed, so you don't want to go too deep."

It was simple enough. I was aided by a tiny pump that worked from a car battery. It fed a hose leading from one of the deeper puddles. Water was used to keep the surface tractable. Each of the prongs on the scratching rake had a wide flat arrowhead. Glyn bent himself down from his considerable height and raked steadily and furiously, scooping great wodges of what seemed like a mix of mud and stones into his sieve. He applied the end of his hose to wash off the sediment and reveal the cockles.

"These are small ones," he said, handing me the sieve and rake. "Try over there."

I bent down. I raked and gathered. I scooped handfuls of lumpy mud soup into my sieve and raked more. I filled it until I could barely lift it. My back was protesting. After a few minutes I had to ease the pain and creaked upwards, reaching for the hose. I doused the mud, which ran away through the wide mesh of the sieve, but as it did so, so did the cockles.

Most of them dropped through.

"Shake them out," said Glyn. So I shook the sieve and hosed in some more water.

The rest of the cockles fell away. I shook hard and washed some more and finally ended up with exactly nine small round shellfish. I didn't want to rattle the sieve again in case they found a way through my mesh.

Glyn peered at my tiny haul. "That's great. Of course, a few years ago we wouldn't have kept tiny ones like that, but we are allowed to now that stocks are good and we can use them."

"Do you eat them yourself?" I asked him as we bounced through the gullies on the way back.

"Well, let's put it this way," he said. "When I was boy if I went to my granny's on a Sunday and I didn't eat them, then I starved."

There are more than 200 species of cockle (even more if you include fossils) with some bizarre names, including the "dog cockle" and the "blood cockle" found in Malaysia, but I wasn't a huge fan. Here was a memory of Welsh childhood. My father loved them. If he could eat custard ice cream (no full cream dairy Vermont cow stuff for Elwyn) and a polystyrene cup of whelks or mussels from a seaside stall, he was on holiday. The nursery food at our table was an echo of his own seaside idyll in Llangrannog.

As a seven year old, I ate anything going too. But the rubbery, grey "little chickens" (as my sister and I called them after the yellow beak-like part of the mollusc) boiled to death and doused in sour vinegar, were like secondhand chewing gum. Perhaps they were better preserved in their tins. According to Glyn, the Spanish now gobbled up ninety percent of the British catch. I decided I would find out if they improved by being cooked in the French fashion with a little wine and onions - "cockles *marinière*".

Before I left Penclawdd we called in at the Roma fish and chip shop. We Welsh, as you may have heard, are "Italians in the rain". And the Italians are all over Wales, in unexpected places, running chip shops, making ice cream and preparing frothy coffi in countless caffis. Given that several square miles of cockle beds lay stretched out in front of the corner chippy on the other side of the sea wall, I asked if they had any cockles.

"Of course. We deep fry them in batter, if that's OK?"

"Sure."

OK? When it came, straight out the fryer, it was cockle popcorn bliss; a tempura heaven. Great batter, sweet cockles, tiny bites. A quid paid

# COCKLES

THE COCKLE HAS AN AVERAGE LIFESPAN OF TWO TO FOUR YEARS, HOWEVER SOME LIVE UP TO NINE YEARS.

---

COCKLES FEED BY FILTERING PLANKTON AND OTHER ORGANIC MATERIALS FROM THE WATER. IT'S SAID THEY CAN FILTER UP TO HALF A LITRE OF WATER PER HOUR.

---

PREDATORS OF THE COCKLE INCLUDE OYSTERCATCHERS, SHORE CRABS, SHRIMPS AND FLATFISH.

---

THE COCKLE MOVES ABOUT BY MEANS OF A MUSCULAR FOOT THAT IT DIGS INTO THE SAND.

---

COCKLE SHELLS HAVE BETWEEN 22 AND 28 RADIATING RIBS AND ARE ALMOST EXACTLY ALIKE.

---

TRADITIONALLY COCKLE PICKING WAS DONE BY WOMEN, AS THE MEN WORKED DOWN THE MINES.

---

THE UK PRODUCES OVER 14,000 TONNES EACH YEAR, WHICH IS ABOUT 150 MILLION COCKLES.

---

COCKLES ARE RICH IN VITAMIN B12 AND ARE A GOOD SOURCE OF PROTEIN.

---

TILL THE END OF THE 19TH CENTURY, PENCLAWDD WAS A BUSY SEAPORT, WITH SEVERAL COAL MINES, AND TINPLATE, COPPER AND BRASS WORKS.

---

THERE WAS ALSO A RAILWAY STATION, A FORGE, 20 GROCERS, 3 BUTCHERS, 3 DRAPERS, 4 FISH AND CHIP SHOPS, 11 PUBS, 3 CHAPELS, A CHURCH AND A CINEMA.

for a huge portion.

In between gazing at the sepia photos on the wall, of big ladies in woolly dresses and head scarves leading donkeys across the marsh, most of whom turned out to be Glyn's aunties, I wandered round the chip shop offering battered cockles to the customers.

Most turned away. "Not cockles, no."

One went as far as "Eeuurgh".

I was disappointed. I thought I had discovered a new craze. It wasn't catching on.

We would leave all the rest to the Spanish then except, perhaps, for a very few for my rugby hero.

## – SHEEP MAY SAFELY… –

Although Weobley Castle is called a "castle", from a technical point of view it's a fortified manor house, and one of the best preserved in Wales. The whole place is essentially a medieval "panic room", thanks to thick fortifying walls, turrets and sturdy gates, but quite a civilised one. "There are galleries, withdrawing rooms and ancient toilets inside," I was told in advance, and I was looking forward to some respite from the dripping weather, except that, when I got there, I discovered that Weobley is a bit of a ruin that Owain Glyndŵr knocked about a bit. It was roofless.

The evening clouds had faded down the grey of the stone. A light drizzle was adding to the gloom. I pulled my coat around my neck and zipped it up tight. I wasn't there for fancy interiors. My quest was out there – on the impressive salt flats, over which Weobley had such a commanding view and over which it might have fired the odd cannon from time to time. It was dusk and the tide was coming in. It was time for a daily mass migration.

I was there to help, to safely gather in the sheep, and then maybe to eat one. There is of course a stereotype about Wales and sheep. It has to be admitted that there are three times as many sheep in Wales as people; nine million to three million. A thousand of this woolly majority were out on these flats. Salt marsh is a great inter-tidal resource. Fish breed there and wading birds nest there, but samphire, sorrel, sea lavender and thrift grow there too. Sheep that chomp on these strongly flavoured herbs of the marshes become flavoursome themselves.

But where were they exactly then in the darkening twilight? I could see nothing.

"Oh, they're off out there somewhere," said Roland and we trudged down a muddy path to the flat lands below. He was pointing ahead to the glistening water. I could make out the odd sheep shape right out in the marshes.

"Surely it's a huge job to get them in?"

Roland was unworried. It was routine. "No, no," he said casually. "They'll come when they see the Land Rover. They want to get to the grass, you understand." He pointed behind me at the startlingly lurid pasture lying directly under the castle.

His son, Will, was driving away from us, very slowly out along a causeway. At the absolute extremity of the rough track, he turned his distant vehicle and then came back at a creeping pace.

The sheep were spread over three hundred acres of damp sludge and tough, juicy herbiage. Now that their secret call had come, they noisily began to clop in towards the central road. They had the distinctly uncertain and nervous manner that sheep maintain whenever they are not actively consuming. With a steady purpose and heads bowed, scattered groups were working their way from distant muddy outposts towards us.

The dogs were there mainly to hassle the strays. They ran out to the extremities. Even though the Land Rover was still way behind, we could see the outriders of the leading mob of sheep coming clearly into view, making their way down to the single gate that led to their evening safety. Except that, about fifty yards away, they halted.

"Oh, they've seen us," said Roland. "They won't want to come through with us standing here." But he didn't move. We watched as the sheep became increasingly fretful. His dog made a wide encirclement to encourage them a little, but that just caused some to bolt to the side: scrambling away across the hundreds of acres of salty bog and disappearing into the drizzle again.

"They don't like *that* you see," Roland pointed at our camera team, "and the camera on legs in particular."

I was parading in a bright red jacket too. We were placed discreetly back from the road, or so we thought, but the herd stopped. The swivel eyes swivelled again and more ran off sideways.

I might have expected Roland to become concerned, but he stood exactly where he was, calmly chatting on about sheep: how the herbs added flavour, how the speed of the tide could be very quick especially on springs, and how the lamb was very popular with French chefs. Meanwhile ever huger numbers of his nervous flock backed up at the bottle neck.

The camera crew slunk backwards into a muddy gully.

Then it happened. A couple ran for it. Two more followed but one went back. Another group chanced it. The noise of baaing and ovine groaning grew ever more insistent. The rest of the flock decided that they would risk it. They started to scissor legs and trot and baa even more loudly. A great racket of sheep-like communication went up and, like a bad encore, suddenly they were all heading for the exit.

"There you are," said Roland matter of factly. "They will all go now." And they did. The stragglers suddenly felt very alone and they ran to catch up. The side-wanderers thought better of their waywardness, the rampant individualists (and sheep are by no means sheep-like) suddenly fancied mass company and they all seemed desperately to need to be in the sloping pasture under the trees.

We turned to watch them. I marvelled at the huge flock crowding up the hill.

"Yes indeed," said Roland, nodding slightly. "I think somebody must have left that lower gate open." He nodded to himself. "They're not supposed to be there in the grounds of the castle, you see."

Typically, Roland didn't seem unduly alarmed. The sheep, like the tide sluicing up Llanelli bay, came in every day. I guess they had done since long before that ancient castle had been there. They would continue to do so, as long as the taste for this special meat from Gower continued to grow. Roland left the sheep and his son to sort themselves out. He got me a leg of lamb from the freezer. I went on my way.

## – RUGBY BALL –

And now to the great game. Ah, the crunch of shoulder blades, the scrape of the ear protector against the bare cheek, the warm embrace of Fatso on your left and Jimpson on the right as the scrum plunged together and collapsed on itself for the third time. I haven't played rugby for 48 years. I haven't been to a Black Sabbath concert either. Yet the same welling conviction that here was my heartland, my identity, my birthright comes back whenever they are mentioned.

I was in East House. We were a soccer house. Most of the school soccer first eleven were drawn from our ranks and, during the spring term, when the squared-off goals were lifted out and replaced by the gaunt "H"s of rugby posts, many of the senior boys were carried away to trounce Bancrofts and Merchant Taylors in a continuing interschool soccer league table.

At that point Mr Cluer would survey the remainder of his flock and nominate fifteen boys to get out there and pretend to be the House First Fifteen.

"Ah, Rhys Jones," he opined. "Your name instantly qualifies you, I think. Hah?" And so, a mere thirteen years old and sporting my "Dixie-Deans" (as my hand-me-down curly-toed football boots were dubbed), I ventured out to do the dirty thing on the rugby field.

We were a feeble crew. Even Savary the school librarian was pressed into service. The gangly, the fat, the knock-kneed, the speccy, the mummy's boy, the lame, the bronchial and the recalcitrant made up East House First Fifteen. The pampered show ponies of the soccer division stood idly by. They sneered at our resounding defeats every Tuesday morning before assembly, but I was game. I felt it my duty as the youngest boy ever to make a House first fifteen to be game. I felt it my duty as the representative of a great Welsh tradition to be game. I felt that diminutive as I was, I had to be game. And I was game: for the entire opposition.

Our feeble company tottered out onto the pitch by the chestnut trees on the other side of Ingrave Road to be utterly and comprehensively pummelled every Wednesday and Saturday afternoon. Rugby forces intimacy with worm-casts. I can still feel the sloppy smear of a full sprawl into the mire of a goal-mouth. I can instantly recall grappling the dank moist clammy leather of a wet ball, and the desperate fumbling attempts to drop kick it out of the way before they all plunged on top of me.

There were no great soaring impromptu male voice choirs for us. It was mud and fighting. I was quite gutsy and I could work up a raging determination, which may ring a few bells with later commissioning editors, but we were no good. No one taught us anything. No one cared. We had to pick it up as we went along. And so when Terry, my Gower rugby hero, declared that he would only join me for dinner if I could kick a goal, this was a severe test of my capabilities.

Terry Davies had been capped for Wales 21 times and even played a handful of times for the British and Irish Lions. He played as a fullback and finished as the leading points scorer on the 1959 British and Irish Lions tour, even though injury restricted him to just 13 of a possible 31 games. He had last played internationally in the sixties. He was eighty now and he had originally come from Llanelli.

I met him at his old school ground. We walked under the trees at the edge of the playing field while he explained how he had been spotted at this very school, how he had played for the reserves and the county and how he had then been offered a place with a nearby team. The difficulty was that that team was Swansea. "I was considered a traitor," he explained.

I had picked up some inkling of this rivalry ten years ago. I was working and staying in the Mumbles. Two matrons passed me near the pier. They stopped me. "Oh, we love your 'Restoration' programme," they said.

I told them that I was disappointed that the great house in Llanelli, a discovery for the programme and a triumph for Wales, had done so badly in the competition. Scotland rallied to its wrecks. Manchester voted en masse for decaying swimming pools. But there just weren't enough Welsh votes to secure this intriguing and beautiful townhouse a place in the final.

They laughed. "We couldn't possibly vote for something in Llanelli."

I looked puzzled.

"We play rugby against Llanelli."

And that was that. Wales is furious in its patriotic antipathy to England but that is nothing compared with the Balkan mistrust of fellow Welshmen. If you want to raise a laugh in Cardiff denigrate Swansea. And Swansea is continually resentful of the unwarranted attention that Cardiff gets. It is even more resentful of warranted attention.

Llanelli was 10 miles away from that conversation in the Mumbles and the Mumbles was the posh bit of Swansea. Satirist Ian Hislop and actress Joanna Page were born there. Catherine Zeta-Jones and Michael Douglas have a house there. Further along the bay, passions ran even higher and dirtier. Terry had had to keep his head down.

He was back in Llanelli now, however, and ready to eat my cockles, but first I had to kick that goal on his old school pitch.

I was never a kicker. Oh, no doubt I had attempted to be. In my house team we were all so incompetent we took it in turns to have a go, but we never got a try so we were seldom put to the test. I dimly recalled that it was sometimes part of my job as a hooker or scrum half (I think I played in both positions) to clear the ball, and this required a drop kick.

I practised in front of Terry. (An incompetent ignoramus trying to prove to a 21-times capped Rugby International that he could "do" his sport.) I could vaguely get a boot under it, though not a good boot, as I was wearing my round-toed multi-laced hill-walking boots.

# RUGBY

WALES ACTUALLY BEGAN THE TRADITION OF SINGING THE NATIONAL ANTHEM BEFORE A GAME WHEN IN 1905 IT WAS DECIDED TO SING THE ANTHEM TO COMPETE WITH THE ALL BLACKS HAKA.

---

WALES WERE THE FIRST NATION TO COMPLETE THE GRAND SLAM WHEN THEY DEFEATED IRELAND IN BELFAST ON MARCH 14TH, 1908.

---

WHEN WALES PLAYED IN BELFAST IN 1908 THEY HAD TO WEAR TRIAL JERSEYS WITHOUT THE PRINCE OF WALES FEATHERS BECAUSE SOMEONE PACKED THE WRONG KIT.

---

THE REIGNING RUGBY OLYMPIC CHAMPIONS ARE THE UNITED STATES. RUGBY HAS ONLY BEEN AN OLYMPIC SPORT FOUR TIMES AND MADE ITS LAST APPEARANCE AT THE 1924 PARIS GAMES.

---

CNAPAN, A ROUGH EARLY FORM OF RUGBY/FOOTBALL PLAYED WITH A SMALL BALL AND BETWEEN TWO LARGE TEAMS, USUALLY FROM NEIGHBOURING PARISHES, WAS PLAYED IN WEST WALES. IT HAD LARGE CHAOTIC SCRUMMAGES, STOPPED AT THE CRY OF "HEDDWCH!" (PEACE) TO AVOID INJURY.

---

RUGBY IS THE NATIONAL SPORT OF 3 COUNTRIES: WALES, NEW ZEALAND AND MADAGASCAR.

---

THE SAME WHISTLE IS USED TO KICK OFF THE OPENING GAME OF EVERY RUGBY WORLD CUP TOURNAMENT. IT IS THE GIL EVANS WHISTLE AND WAS FIRST BLOWN BY GIL EVANS FROM SWANSEA, WHO OVERSAW A MATCH BETWEEN ENGLAND AND NEW ZEALAND IN 1905.

Terry undertook to coach me. He started to mark out the kick. The angle was 90 degrees to the post. It was a straightforward hoof. I had to get lift and a straight path to the trajectory.

Terry placed the ball and carefully instructed me. "Take three steps," he said. "Two back, and one to the side. And as you hit the ball lean into it a bit and it will rise up."

I stood back, measured the distance, waited for the camera to turn over and then walked forwards, as casually as possible and kicked the ball exactly as instructed. Yes, the ball lifted. It soared straight over the crossbar and through the posts.

This wasn't exactly what we wanted. It would have been more useful if I had missed dismally four or five times. But I did really hit it in one. Terry was ready for his supper. We just needed a couple more angles.

It took another ten kicks before I managed to do it again. And that was because, try as I might, I never quite took it as slowly and methodically as I had the first time. I rushed at it. I put too much effort in. I swung wildly. I sweated and flailed. It's just like golf. As long as I abandoned all ambition and simply walked it with as little effort as possible, the ball shot straight over the bar. But I had to follow my instructions.

## – WELL DONE –

The salt-marsh lamb was roasted. The cockles were cooked in a little wine and herbs, exactly as I would cook mussels. I fried the onions in butter, boiled the wine and added the shellfish, waiting until they opened of their own accord before serving. Terry said he loved them, but he didn't eat many. The lamb, however, he devoured. We did it all in the kitchen of a smart new restaurant in an old tin factory in the remains of Llanelli docks, owned, as it happened, by two more rugby heroes, Stephen Jones and Dwayne Peel. Had I needed to, perhaps, I would have had a choice of subjects. This corner of Wales has produced some of the finest rugby players our country has seen, including Shane Williams, Leigh Halfpenny and the legendary 'Merv the Swerv' Davies. But I liked Terry best. I don't think anybody could have taught me to kick a goal with such grace and charm. It was a result.

I felt long-forgotten Welsh rugby connections warming the cockles of my heart.

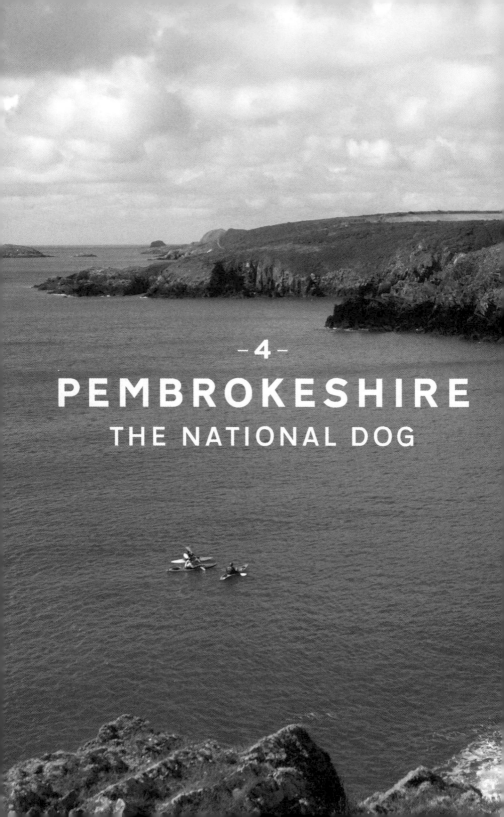

# – 4 –
# PEMBROKESHIRE
## THE NATIONAL DOG

# – TIPI OR NOT TIPI –

If you press out and away from St Davids, that tiny cathedral city on the very tip of Pembrokeshire, you soon leave the crowded tourist trail behind. The coastal path runs on for over 150 miles, around the whole county seaboard, passing 58 beaches and 14 harbours. It constantly offers up surprises: a sudden stony bay, a jutting mound of an island, a flower-strewn, exposed headland, or even a tipi.

Around Strumble Head, nearer to Fishguard, several different aeons of time collide on the geological map. It erupts in identifying colours: red for Ordovician, bright green for Cambrian, yellow for pre-Cambrian. Intrusive igneous or burnt stone competes for space with limestone deposits and volcanic sedimentary rock. Between 650 and 290 million years old, they swirl solidly beneath the flattened gorse and strangely shaped boulders. Wherever this stone breaks through in the jagged hill "castles" there are signs of ancient habitation, with fallen walls and standing stones. Somehow, it's not totally surprising to climb over Garn Fechan and find a tipi encampment on the other side.

John, a local small-holder in Trefasser has erected three "Native American tipis" to tempt New Age tourists. Original Native American tipis were anything up to 16 foot tall and required 12 buffalo hides to cover them. When tipis were originally constructed they were built with the door facing east towards the sun to protect against prevailing winds. John's were covered with white canvas and had rough hessian covering for a floor, a bed and some basic furniture.

He had a hot tub too. He showed me how he could fill the bottom with logs. I guess you have to avoid sitting in the hot spot. A ring of stones had been hauled together to surround a camp fire. During the high season John turned people away. But today there was a slight chill. The summer visitors, drawn to Pembrokeshire by the beaches, had gone. In 2010 there were four million of them. The tourism industry is worth more than half a billion pounds. Today, though, the choughs were bundling over the black rock. The sea was flecked with white. Sheep were huddling under the earth banks. I settled by the fire and, pulling at my clothes, I discovered my quest. It was pretty simple. I had to "walk a Corgi" – the Welsh national dog.

# PEMBROKESHIRE FACTS.

THE HIGHEST KNOWN MONTHLY
SUNSHINE TOTAL IN WALES IS 354.3 HOURS
RECORDED AT DALE FORT (PEMBROKESHIRE)
IN JULY 1955.

MATHEMATICIAN ROBERT RECORDE
OF PEMBROKESHIRE INVENTED
THE "EQUALS" SIGN.

PEMBROKESHIRE-BORN BARTHOLOMEW ROBERTS
IS CONSIDERED THE MOST SUCCESSFUL
PIRATE OF THE GOLDEN AGE OF PIRACY AND IS
THOUGHT TO HAVE BEEN THE FIRST PIRATE TO NAME
HIS FLAG "JOLLY ROGER", IN JUNE 1721.

MILK PRODUCTION IN PEMBROKESHIRE
INCREASED GREATLY AFTER WWII. PRE-WAR
THE AREA PRODUCED AROUND 9 MILLION
GALLONS OF MILK, BY 1948 THE FIGURE
WAS CLOSE TO 20 MILLION.

IN THE 1950s GRASS IN PEMBROKESHIRE
WAS BEING RAVAGED BY RABBITS WHEN
IT WAS ESTIMATED THAT THERE WERE FOUR
TO FIVE MILLION RABBITS ON
PEMBROKESHIRE FARMS.

To begin, we headed off to Jack Pontiago's garage near Llanwnda. I own a cottage in this area. I have driven past his workshop, amongst the fields at the bottom of the hill a hundred times, and have often slowed down to admire a rank of fading Morris Minors on the grass.

These old motors, standing in front of a painted, breeze-block workshop, bolted onto the corrugated hay barn, where Jack started his car business 60 years ago, weren't collectors' items. This wasn't a dealership. The rounded bonnets were matte with age. The chrome was tarnished. Some had collapsed, like broken barns. Some had sunk onto their wheel hubs.

And here they were, in close-up. One was a scratched blue, another a scuffed grey and a third was a Morris Traveller, the estate version, with the whole of the rear section and its painted wooden frame fallen into an utter state of collapse. It was a green one, exactly like the family car we had when I was very little, with its pop eyes and yellow wooden superstructure; the one that Bella the black French poodle viciously guarded, the one we took to visit Cardiff. On this wreck, that wood was now faded white and bursting with rot-encrusted fungus. The thing lay on its axles. The number plate (valuable in itself, I would have thought, to any passing Adrian) read "ADE 130".

There was only one workable Morris there. Jack had just serviced that particular pale blue bumblebee with an MOT. It was a family heirloom. "A local car," Jack said, "but the owner passed away and now his son has it in Llanelli." (A foreign country, by the sound of it, and a long way to come with an old car.)

Sporting a jaunty navy-blue corduroy hat, Jack escorted me around his domain. He loved his battered charges. "They purr," he said jovially. He proclaimed the virtues of their simple mechanics and the straightforward engine, which, set down over the front axle, apparently made for an unexpected nimbleness.

The designer, Sir Alec Issigonis, was later responsible for that other world-straddling, mass-market little car: the Mini. With the Morris Minor, however, Sir Alec had apparently decided, at the last minute, that the car was too narrow. Jack fondly patted a square flat ridge down the front of the bonnet. "He cut it in half and added an extra four inches here," he explained. During development, it was called the "Morris Mosquito", a reference to the warplane and a reminder that the car was conceived in an austere age of rationing. "I just love these cars," said Jack.

Others did too. It sold a million by 1961 and continued in production into the early seventies. It helped make the fortune of William Morris, Lord Nuffield, who had started with a small business mending bicycles, not unlike Jack Pontiago himself.

Jack escorted me over the road to show me his great-grandfather's workshop: a blacksmith's forge where he still mended tractors. He handed me an object, like a perforated or louvered tin can. "You know that, don't you?"

I shook my head.

"It's a headlight blackout cover we made for the cars in the Second World War," Jack chortled.

Back then most of Jack's work was for farms. Most of the machinery he mended still involved horses.

The farmers, out on this huge peninsula, where the mountains of Wales rolling down from the north had been flattened by a distant Ice Age, must have liked the Morris Minor. When my wife and I dug out the wheel pit in a nearby mill (where I am writing this now) we discovered a complete little car crushed flat at the bottom. I wondered if Jack would have accepted it, even as a Morris sandwich. He said he was still up for more (he once had twenty-two in his collection) and would take another "as long as my wife is not looking out from the bedroom window." Jack gestured across the road at a smart house with a bright green lawn, where, sitting chewing at a ball, was what appeared to be a Corgi dog.

I laughed. This wasn't expected. My search was over. Yes, it was a Corgi, called Macsen. We walked over. "Can I walk him?" I asked Jack.

"No," he replied, skewering my hopes. "He won't have a collar. When he was little he pulled his head right out of one. It must have hurt his ears and ever since we can't get near him."

Macsen, named for a character in the *Mabinogion*, snarled at me from the other side of the gate. I leaned down to get a closer look at him. He started frothing and snapping, wrestling with an eternal canine dilemma. He wanted me to throw his spittle-slimed ball. But he didn't want to let me have the thing.

"He's always had a short fuse, this one," Jack explained. "We've had Corgis for years."

"All like this?"

"No, no, the rest of them have been very friendly. They're a good family dog, you know."

Macsen bared his teeth and growled.

"How do you walk him?"

"We don't. He just runs around in the garden and barks at the cars. It keeps him fit enough." Macsen was a Pembrokeshire Corgi. There were Cardiganshire Corgis too. But the locally developed breed had a foxier face, pointier ears and no tail.

My father's family had had Corgis, I remembered. I never threw balls for them and I don't know what type they were. It was all in the distant days of tennis clubs and leafy suburbs, growing up in smart Llanishen near Cardiff. The Corgi had become the Welsh canine badge of office. My father's, fondly remembered throughout his life, was called "Twp" – which means "stupid", apparently.

None of this was encouraging. Perhaps I had been given the wrong dog. Pembrokeshire had also produced the Sealyham Terrier. Were they less stupid or bonkers? That Welsh breed for a while had become the Hollywood lap dog of choice for, amongst others, Alfred Hitchcock, Richard Burton, Elizabeth Taylor, Humphrey Bogart and Bette Davis. It was also a favourite of the Queen Mother and Princess Margaret. But now they were very rare.

Perhaps everybody had Corgis now. Macsen was clearly not going to play ball. I needed to look elsewhere.

## – NIPPER –

"The Corgi dog was bred for cattle breeding," Andrew the vet explained later that day. (He practised in Fishguard – "doing a bit of town and a bit of country".) "It is a tough diminutive big dog, not a lap dog," he went on. "It was bred to herd cows. It doesn't circle the herd like a sheep dog. It runs up and down behind it and nips at the ankles."

The Corgi's low stature helped them roll out of the way of a good kicking.

Picking me up at Hugh's farm down near Llanwnda, Andrew was driving me across the open, distinctive North Pembrokeshire landscape. His Land Cruiser was his refuge. He used it to escape from a wild day out of doors, dealing with stock in this weatherbeaten world.

"In fact the climate is mild. That's what makes the rearing of farm animals so successful. You get a longer grass-growing season. But the wind blows hard."

The south-western coastal strip of Pembrokeshire manages an

average annual sunshine total of over one thousand seven hundred hours, but the region can get more than thirty "force 8" gales a year. We were rumbling past that other notable mark of this landscape – the blasted tree, creeping cautiously up out of a mud-and-stone hedge bank into a stunted, leaning plume of tangled, inter-growing twig hair rocking in the breeze.

From the top of rocky Garn Fawr, standing in the tantalising remains of a 3,000-year-old village encampment known as an Iron Age fort and probably more village than castle, it was possible to look down and see the way that the land had been divided 2,500 years ago for cattle.

The field boundaries still ran away from the defensive site like the spokes of a wheel, so that each of the ancient villagers would have possessed marshland down by the stream, some good grazing land on the gentle slopes and stony stuff nearer the top. There were ancient cattle drifts to get them in for milking, and, if you looked for them, the remains of corrals: round-walled, circular enclosures built by the Britons to keep their herds safe from raiders.

Cattle is still the deal round here, with recent statistics showing that there are over 1,000,000 of them in Wales. The original Welsh black cattle of this area predated the Romans. "Though they were not actually black, in those days," Andrew explained. "They bred the various browns and whites out of them in modern times."

He meant over the last 200 years. The "Iron Age", the "Dark Ages" and the long, settled existence before we started mechanising farm life, may seem to blend into one, but it represents 6,000 years of slow, gentle evolution and adaptation. Those Iron Age field boundaries are still in use.

Above Hugh's farm, where I met Andrew, with his hand up a cow, checking her ovulation status, there is a little-visited burial site. A great flat boulder has been propped open like a yawning shell just under the rocky summit of a hill. Sitting by it, the land drops away for a mile to the granite cliff and the edge of the St George's Channel. A warrior, or king, or notable chieftain was buried there 5,000 years ago, with a view across to Ireland; but not a soothing one. It's a blood-stirring vista that looks out to the grey tumbling ocean and reminds us that Pembrokeshire is an exposed wedge of land in a cold sea.

The Llanwnda memorial chamber also looks down on the site of the last invasion of Britain in 1797. The dregs of the Brest and Le Havre jails who made up this invasion force were finally cowed into surrender by a phantom army of Welsh women in their red shawls. This is a legend. Except that it also appears to be true. Napoleonic revolutionary generals had imagined that the peasants of the west would rise up against their English oppressors, but the land was rich and the peasants were tenant farmers, wealthy enough to want to see off the Frog. Over the next 50 years, many of them took shares in ships that traded out of nearby Fishguard. Two hundred years ago, these were prosperous men.

Andrew's job, as a vet, was to ensure that modern husbandry was prosperous too, but he felt that efficiency was becoming farming's own worst enemy. "They struggle," he told me. "The prices are always being driven down by the supermarkets, and the margins become less viable all the time." The agricultural work force fell by around two thirds between 1871 and 1969. Where once a small farm might have supported the family and nine or ten others, spread around cottages in the fields, now the farms needed to amalgamate. A father and son could look after 250 acres or more with a tractor and harvester. They needed Andrew's expert advice to run these bigger farms successfully. These days he was as much concerned with prediction and prevention as he was with cure.

"There could not be a more welcoming bunch," he said. "They have always been so warm to me." He was originally from Cardiff. (Not as many cows there.) He particularly loved the sea off the beaches in Pembrokeshire. He kayaked and surfed. But he was many years away from being accepted as a local. After all, the king of the Morris Minors, Jack Pontiago, actually lived in Pontiago. Jack carried the name of his own village: not something that a newcomer could easily aspire to.

Andrew's spoken Welsh was not great, he confessed. He understood more than he talked. Pembrokeshire has a line across its middle, guarded by castles. Below it is the Englishry, occupied and colonised by the Normans and Flemish, where the English language is traditionally spoken. In this part of North Pembrokeshire, however, Welsh is the first language. One of my problems with Macsen was that Macsen understood no English at all. The only commands that the very Welsh dog understood were Welsh ones. It was a portent.

## – FISHGUARD UPPERS –

Hedydd lived on Strumble Head too. She called the Welsh language she spoke "the language of Heaven". It was her first tongue. "When you want to make a programme about that you should come and see me again," she said.

# AGRICULTURE

FARMING AND AGRICULTURE
WERE THE PRIMARY INDUSTRY IN
PEMBROKESHIRE IN THE 19TH CENTURY
WHEN NEARLY 130,000 PEOPLED
WORKED IN THE INDUSTRY
(38% OF THE TOTAL WORKFORCE).

---

DURING THIS PERIOD MILK
PRODUCTION ACCOUNTED FOR
OVER HALF THE INCOME OF FARMING,
WITH THE REVENUE FROM MILK
EXCEEDING £4 MILLION.

---

MIGRATION TO THE CITIES AND
NEW TECHNOLOGY HIT THE
AREA HARD. THE AGRICULTURAL
LABOUR FORCE FELL 71%
BETWEEN 1871 AND 1969.

---

PEMBROKE FARMER'S CLUB IS THE
SECOND OLDEST IN THE UK.

We were to meet on a bench in Lower Fishguard harbour. First we had to film the place.

There are two Fishguards: Upper and Lower. It is difficult to sort out which is the lovelier and which the more ruined by traffic. Many of the smaller Welsh towns have missed out on spanking new shopping centres and traffic calming schemes. Of course Welsh councils are councils and they long to catch up. They are only restricted from "modernising" by lack of funds. But instead of building new cul-de-sacs and "modern" bleak housing estates on the outskirts, they could save these wonderful places if they restored them and then completely sealed them off from cars (like modern housing estates). The refurbished centres could become close-quartered living areas.

Some hope. The little village of Lower Fishguard straddles the main road along the coast so closely that people have actually abandoned the houses on either side of it. If you turn away towards the sea though, and venture further from the road, you will find a long, tidal quay sitting quietly under high cliffs, and the best view of this sublime harbour is from Upper Fishguard, on the other side of the bay. Tudor and Chris and Gary had set up on one of the footpaths that snake along the far cliff and I tried to find them. "We're in front of the houses," they told me on the radio.

"Which houses?'

"You take a right past the cinema and then right again."

"OK. Let me sort this. We took a right by the deli, and I left the car in the car park down there. I thought you were along here."

"I think we're probably somewhere above you."

I thought so too, but an impenetrable wall of gorse and bracken blocked the way. I wasn't going back. And I certainly wasn't asking for directions. I was a late middle-aged man. I don't ask. And I wasn't clambering through the brambles. I could find them. Ten minutes later (a long time in television filming terms) and a flight of concrete steps I finally did.

"This is a great view of Lower Fishguard."

"The view down there is even better."

"We're higher."

They were indeed, and now we were gazing down on the row of pretty fisherman's cottages and the quay and the cliff rising up on the other side. Few towns as underrated as Fishguard can boast such vistas. It was why it became a film star.

# FISHGUARD

THE NAME DERIVES FROM OLD NORSE
FISKIGAR MEANING "FISH CATCHING ENCLOSURE",
INDICATING THAT THERE MAY HAVE BEEN A
SCANDINAVIAN TRADING POST, BUT NO EVIDENCE
HAS BEEN FOUND. IT WAS CALLED "FISCARD" UNTIL
THE TURN OF THE 19TH CENTURY.

FISHGUARD WAS FAMOUS FOR EXPORTING
SALT, OATS AND HERRING, BUT TRADE
FELL AWAY AND IN 1883 ONLY SIX SHIPS
SAILED FROM FISHGUARD WITH CARGO.

WHEN FIRST GREAT WESTERN MOVED THE
IRISH FERRY TRAFFIC FROM NEYLAND
TO FISHGUARD IN THE EARLY 20TH CENTURY
THE POPULATION OF FISHGUARD MORE THAN
DOUBLED OVER THE COURSE OF 20 YEARS.

THE LAST INVASION OF BRITAIN TAPESTRY
THAT ILLUSTRATES THE BATTLE OF FISHGUARD
WAS CREATED BY OVER 70 WOMEN IN 1997. IN TOTAL
IT IS 30 METRES LONG AND TOOK FOUR YEARS TO
DESIGN AND SEW. 94 DIFFERENT COLOURS OF
STITCHING WERE USED IN ITS CREATION.

# – FILM FUN –

John Huston's "Moby Dick" was filmed in Fishguard first, or some small part of it. Huston, living in Ireland at the time, was apparently unwilling to fly back to the States, and so chose Wales as a stand-in for Nantucket. (He also employed Ireland and a bit of Guinea as well.) New Bedford and the East Coast of America had become heavily industrialised so Huston sought a "port that hadn't changed materially for the last hundred years".

Mind you, Nantucket is a flat, featureless, empty sandbank off New York while Fishguard is an ancient, cliff-bound rocky cove. Huston admitted later that, despite writing the screenplay, he had never "been able to read the damn book". It might not have made much difference. Melville the author had never visited Nantucket, or Wales, for that matter. The film was "the most difficult picture I ever made" Huston said later. It was originally budgeted at $3 million but went over to around $4.5 million because of the expense of moving the production from Portugal to Ireland, then to Wales and then the Canaries. Whether much of the quay and the area featured in the epic film it is difficult to tell, but Gregory Peck definitely hung out in Fishguard. He entranced the local women with his beautiful dancing, so they say.

Fifteen years later, in 1971, Peter O'Toole and Richard Burton rolled into town to make the film of "Under Milk Wood". The fictional name of the town was "Llareggub", which spelled backwards reads "bugger all". The director of "Under Milk Wood", Andrew Sinclair, donated the rights for the 1972 movie "to the Welsh nation" with the hope of raising funds for cultural projects in Wales.

"Only Fools and Horses" star David Jason played a role in the film, and this time the locals were included too. Hedydd and her sister had the part of little sisters looking into a sweet shop window.

"I remember they gave me a tuppenny bit," she said when I sat next to her on the bench on the quay.

I was older than Hedydd. "Was there a tuppeny bit?" I asked "I only recall a threepenny bit." Decimalisation had ruined everything. It had certainly ruined me. Why was I being so pedantic? The whole thing was a fantasy, after all.

Hedydd vividly remembered waking up in the night, looking out of her bedroom window and seeing an actor riding a pig outside the pub. This was a dream sequence in the film. The whole visit ultimately remained a dream for the local community. The film people came in all their fashionable clothes, with their huge amounts of money and transformed the quayside, making shops where there were no shops, and building new extensions to the village where there was no village. Then they went.

There are no shops now, no pigs and only one pub. It seems inconceivable that Lower Fishguard has survived so simply. No gift shop, not even a café. No ice cream placards or tables and chairs on the dockside. It is a little miracle. Except for the rumble and screech of lorries descending to the minute bridge across the Gwaun and grinding up the cliff on the other side, Lower Fishguard is quiet.

Elizabeth Taylor never made it to Lower Fishguard. Rosie Probert (Taylor's character) recorded all her bits in a studio in West London. Richard Burton was entranced. "If this were in the Mediterranean," he is reported to have said, "it would be the most successful holiday resort in the world."

He planned to bring his yacht and his lovely bride back. He even boasted that he had the ideal vehicle for exploring the hills: a Mini Moke that lived aboard the boat. But he never came and Lower Fishguard never became famous. I was pleased. And I sensed that Hedydd was too.


## – COASTEERING MOOD –


The cove at Lower Fishguard looks like an exposed harbour to me, but it doesn't get much swell, or so Hedydd told me. This is because of the great breakwater that stretches out from Goodwick on the other side of the wider bay to provide a deepwater quay for the Irish Ferry. It was originally built to take Atlantic liners. A few came, including the *Lusitania*, but then the war intervened and they stuck with Liverpool. During World War Two, two ships from the port (the *St David* and the *St Andrew*) were used to help rescue soldiers from Dunkirk.

Pembrokeshire is well supplied with shelter. Further down the coast, the deep inlet of Milford Haven is the fourth largest port in Britain in terms of overall tonnage, and the busiest of all for "oil products", but most of the little harbours look frightening. To land Vikings, or to fend off a French invasion, or to carry off bricks from Porthgain, brave skippers had to point their ships straight at the cliffs of Pembrokeshire, and seek out the tiny coves and sea walls that would keep the crashing sea out of the harbour while they tied up for a tide that would leave them high and dry and praying for good weather to get them back out.

I sometimes run along a section of the coastal path near Strumble Head. My wife is convinced that I will slip and tumble to my death. What a way to go. The path squiggles past buttresses and overlooks sudden drops to the sea. I love the recurring incident, the hard stony beaches clad in grey pebbles and littered with wreckage worn smooth by the breakers, but I have only seen one side of the spectacle. "Coasteering" offered the other.

I wasn't looking forward to it. I am a former fatty. In gymnastics at school I had to cry in order to get off being forced to climb a rope. I have sailed a few boats and now I am constantly expected to leap or dangle or clamber for TV programmes. They want me to fall off, of course. The only thing that drives me on is that I have no intention of doing so.

Imagination is my enemy. I was imagining how cold that sea was going to be. I was imagining how agonising climbing about sharp rocks on my knees would be. On a grey day in September, I went to get kitted out. I was imagining how uncomfortable that kit would be.

"You can leave your clothes on the hook."

Just the smell of the changing room depressed me.

"There's your wet suit."

As I slurped and farted into the thing I got more and more self-pitying, tearing the cold rubber up over hairy calves and then trying to calm the folds of intractable tyre-like black gloop around my stomach. There is a long zip up the back with a big drawstring on it which I can never reach. God, I didn't even have the strength to pull that up.

I cheered up a bit when I saw what lift and separation the black stuff achieved. I felt smoothed out and positively svelte. It's a little bit fetishistic.

The instructor Jon came in. "You need to wear one of these," he said. And he handed me a pair of Hawaii print beach shorts. "They cover your modesty."

"What modesty?"

"St Davids is a conservative place."

I looked down. I was a series of smooth planes in significant areas. There was no indication of anything untoward.

"But they are mostly to protect our wet suits."

I put on the flower-bedecked Bermudans. And then I was naff again.

After the addition of a life jacket and silly helmet, we had to walk along a cliff to get to a path down to the ocean.

The camera doesn't like boats. Boats wobble too much. I knew the filming would be difficult. I started descending internally. Is it a Welsh trait, this moodiness? I might even equate it with the lie of the land. Always up or down, never flat. Perhaps it's not Welsh, it's just me. By the time we were ten minutes away from my autumnal immersion I had become sullen.

Rachel was there to instruct me. She regularly took people out doing this, even in February. I avoided her gaze.

"Are you looking forward to it?" she enquired chirpily.

"It's just a job," I replied morosely.

Oh dear. Forgive me, Rachel. Yes, intolerable. Still, it made me feel better. And you are so very attractive.

We poised by the sea edge, perched on an outcrop. There weren't many big waves. Jon had predicted that, with the wind in the north, the swell under the cliff would be slight. He was right. The sun came out. The boat with the camera aboard chugged around the corner. It was a big, stable rib. Tudor was secure and happy with his platform. The cliffs were steep. It could motor close to the cliffs. There was no reason for the pictures to wobble unduly.

By the time we jumped in I was on the upward trend again. As soon as we had swum across to the next outcrop, I had forgotten my Hawaiian shorts. As we clambered up on a ledge, I had become friendly towards my helmet and life jacket. This was really extraordinarily jolly. We traversed cliff faces, plunged into the water, paddled a few more feet and found another rock to heave ourselves out on. The wet suit was warm. The climbing was playground stuff. The leaping took me back to Harlow Pool.

There was a disgusting object called a Lion's Mane jellyfish. I had to swim carefully around it, but I was interested to hear that, though excruciatingly painful to bump into inadvertently, it was a rarity. And the cliffs and stones were now revealing themselves in glorious close-up, as they never could from their summits.

We splashed across the bay to a monstrous pyramid of a rock, its granite pressed into level slabs of purple stone, and then lifted sideways, making a massive sculptural fist in the sea. This was like going rock-pooling when you were a kid, without a mother standing there telling you to be careful. This was a wild Welsh experience. This was great.

Perhaps I will become a hard tough guy sitting in the corner after all. In the meantime they hauled me out and landed me at St Non's Bay to wade ashore where St David the evangelist was reputedly born and baptised by St Elvis.

# – DING, DANG, DUNG –

I had a moment or two to collect myself and then wandered up through the tiny bleak little cathedral city of St Davids and out into the drab bungalow suburbs.

I crossed a field of black cattle to join Sarah Beynon. She was taking me to inspect her latest research project. Arranged in a small corner of a paddock was a series of neatly spaced holes about six inches across. A wire net sat on top of the holes and on top of that sat a round cake of brown matter.

"I made them all myself," Sarah said proudly. "They are dung cakes."

She made the traps too. The cakes looked like those elephant droppings that the artist Chris Ofili uses to prop up his canvases. Each was a smoothly rounded ball of cowpat: a tempting sphere the size of a cricket ball.

Tempting, that is, were you a dung beetle. Sarah had set up an elaborate trap. The beetles were attracted to the dung. They strode towards it, rattling the 30 plates of their shiny armour, and would then fall through the wire and into the top of a pink plastic funnel.

Sarah had cut off the lower pipe of the funnels to enable them to tumble into a black plastic flower pot with some grass in it; not so much grass that they could clamber out, but enough to provide shelter. Sarah had no intention of stressing her beetles.

The whole project seemed a work of art to me, like an installation in the Tate (alongside Mr Ofili, perhaps). In fact its serious purpose was to measure the incidence of dung beetles, and then to put a monetary value to them. "We want to know what financial contribution a dung beetle makes to animal husbandry," Sarah explained.

Dung beetles do a necessary, natural job – clearing dung, redistributing it and fertilising the soil. Here in this paddock in Pembrokeshire where the mild weather provided abundant growth, where natural systems still dominated, here in organic farmland, she wanted to try and find out the number of beetles per acre and estimate the work they did, and so had set up her delicate hunting machinery.

"Put your hand in and see whether there are any there," she prompted.

African dung beetles are television celebrities, purposefully rolling balls of camel poo towards their burrows. There is little we like better than a hardworking insect. We would let our daughters marry one. What worthy planetary citizens these tumblebugs or dung chafers are. But the ones I remembered were African: huge, I expect. I stuck my hand into the

# AROUND ST DAVID'S

PRIOR TO THE MINES AND COLLIERIES ACT
OF 1842, A HIGHER PROPORTION OF WOMEN HAD
WORKED UNDERGROUND IN THE PEMBROKESHIRE
MINES THAN ANYWHERE IN BRITAIN WITH 42%
OF THE WORKFORCE BEING FEMALE.

PEMBROKESHIRE WAS STRATEGICALLY PLACED
DURING WWII TO COMMAND THE MAIN SHIPPING
ROUTES AND PLAYED A MAJOR PART IN THE FIGHT
AGAINST GERMAN SUBMARINES.

IN THE EARLY 20TH CENTURY THERE WAS AN
EXTRAORDINARILY HIGH PERCENTAGE OF YOUNG
PEOPLE IN THE COUNTY WITH THE 1901 CENSUS
REPORTING THAT 43% OF THE POPULATION WERE
UNDER 20 YEARS OLD.

IN THE 19TH CENTURY CALDEY ISLAND
WAS KNOWN FOR EXPORTING LIMESTONE,
WITH 20,000 TONS BEING SHIPPED FROM
THERE A YEAR.

SKOKHOLM ISLAND BECAME THE UK'S
FIRST OFFICIAL BIRD RESERVE IN 1933.

THE HMS WARRIOR, WHICH WAS THE WORLD'S
FIRST FULLY ARMOURED WARSHIP, WAS DOCKED
IN MILFORD HAVEN FOR 50 YEARS BETWEEN
1930 AND 1980.

pot where something was scuttling. There were six beetles in there.

OK. They were pretty big too.

The British dung beetle is not only a physical match for the African but shares its appetite. Dung is all they need. They don't drink. They won't eat anything else. They are poop-mad. They just consume dung and help cows by clearing up the field, by naturally distributing the fertiliser and by removing a source of cow irritation: flies. And, considering their trade, they scrub up well.

How remarkably sparkly, clean and efficiently accoutered these horny beetles seemed: these relatives of the Egyptian scarab. They walked off determinedly, as beetles must when they are disturbed, and I had to keep gently guiding them back into my palm.

Scientists in South Africa and Sweden recently showed that dung beetles use the stars for orientation and navigation, making them the first animal proven to use the Milky Way this way. But glancing round I suddenly realised that, to have so many in just one of these little holes, the field must be seething with their relatives.

"They're strong too," said Sarah, who was obviously besotted with the creatures. "Clasp your other hand over them."

I made a cup.

"Can you feel it?" She asked. And I could. The beetles were pushing with their legs, trying to break out, and the force was quite disproportionate to their size. They can pull over one thousand times their body weight. Were they human they would be able to haul six double-decker buses up the street.

Is "Dung Beetle-Man" coming to Marvel Comics soon? Some sort of superhero shit-shoveller is what we need. But here was a strong scientific basis for the maintenance of the continuing natural order in Wales. An indiscriminate use of pesticides was killing off these natural allies. A single cow can produce seven tons of dung a year. Sarah wanted to remind us to put our faith in beetles. I was a convert.

– HAVERFORDWEST –

Haverfordwest is worth walking. Some of its inhabitants nurse a sense of growing despair over the future of this hill-straddling, wonderful market town. Evelyn Waugh, stationed nearby during World War Two, admired its simple dignity and elegant buildings, calling it "a town of great beauty", but the necessary pomposity that once accrued to its local status has been undermined. There are important churches, and a ruined castle and former prison dominate one hill. As I threaded through the back streets, making my way to a church hall near St Mary's on the other, I passed the old courthouse and assembly rooms, now a café. I passed the shuttered grand town villas designed by John Nash, now empty. The commercial centre of the town had shifted to the riverside and a jumble of ill-designed shopping precincts.

I had met with the Civic Society. In fact, as I recall, I am a member of the Civic Society, and they had pointed out the threats to the fabric of the town. "You know what you need," I ventured, with foolish authority, "A Townscape Heritage Initiative, to preserve the outside appearance of this high street." There was silence. Someone deftly tried to change the subject. Eventually, another member gently said, "We have already had one of those."

But people do still live in the middle of Haverfordwest. I followed an old pedestrian passage that led up to steps that crept, under heavy limes, behind St Thomas's Church to the door of the St Thomas's Church Hall, where I had been told to go. I peered in. There was a short corridor and another open door gave onto a church hall, which was now filled with dozens of dogs.

## – CORGI TOYS –

The Pembrokeshire Canine Association was gathered for a "ring craft session". I had rather expected that I would be visiting a rough instruction course for errant family pets: perhaps a few puppies, or people trying to get their own Macsen to behave on walks, but these were serious owners with serious dogs. There were pedigree whippets, retrievers, German Shepherds, poodles, pugs: all clearly of dog show standard.

These were the best of their respective breeds. Their owners were beyond being taught how to get Fido to stay off the sofas. They were encouraging Fidolatrus Hargreaves Rapscallion the Third to walk properly, to turn in a neat circle and to endure the indignity of being stood on a table while a judge poked at his teeth and felt his bone structure.

And there were Corgis here. There were at least six Corgis. I sat to one side with the owner of three, Sue Bale, while other dogs marched around in front of me. Sue told me how her pampered charges were billeted down in their own kennel area. She was breeding to try to achieve a winner, off the back of a purchase made originally in England. Her great hope was young Merlin, not one of the older ones at all, but a puppy, now just reaching the age when he might be taken to show rings.

We stood Merlin on a little table and Eileen demonstrated all his good points. His regular jaw, his strong shoulders, his scissor bite, his flat skull, his slightly rounded ears, his black-rimmed eyes, his perfect proportions.

The Corgi (or "dwarf dog" in Welsh, "ci" meaning dog and "cor" meaning dwarf) is by no means a lap dog. It is short but strong and "robust", and is said to have come over to Pembrokeshire with the Flemish in the twelfth century, but being a rough working dog, the Corgi didn't get into the actual showroom until 1925. Now it is a recognised breed. Welsh folklore says that Corgis were used by fairies and elves to pull their coaches, or to serve as the steeds for their warriors. A visible "saddle" in the fur on the back is another good point that breeders look for.

Later, I prepared to take Merlin for a walk in the park. This was my moment. This was what I had been asked to do. I had seen the cattle, I had examined their dung, I had met their vets and walked their countryside. Now I had to fit in the final piece of the puzzle and meet a proper Pembrokeshire working dog.

Two of the regular judges from local shows stood to one side in the late evening light. I knew what I had to do. I had to march my faithful companion down to a small stand of trees, turn him and walk him back.

It was important to keep Merlin focused and trotting in a straight line by my side. I had to get him to turn in a nice curve and I had now learned that I had to keep his alert attention by whistling, peeping, calling his name and yapping furiously all the time.

Alas, I quickly ran out of noises that interested him. He wouldn't respond to the ones he had already heard. Merlin got bored with his parade and when I got back to the judges he refused to sit quietly and especially to stare at me in rapt admiration, as he was supposed to.

Merlin was young and I was a novice. But Corgis are simply not that easy to take for a walk, not properly anyway. I liked Merlin. Merlin was indifferent to me.

So, despite finding a real Pembrokeshire Corgi, a potential champion of the breed to boot, despite his charming nature, despite my lessons, despite my bright eyes and fluffy demeanour, the judges were not impressed. I completely failed to walk the dog properly. Honestly, you know what they say. "Never work with…"

– 5 –

# MID WALES
## A LEGEND IN THE MAKING

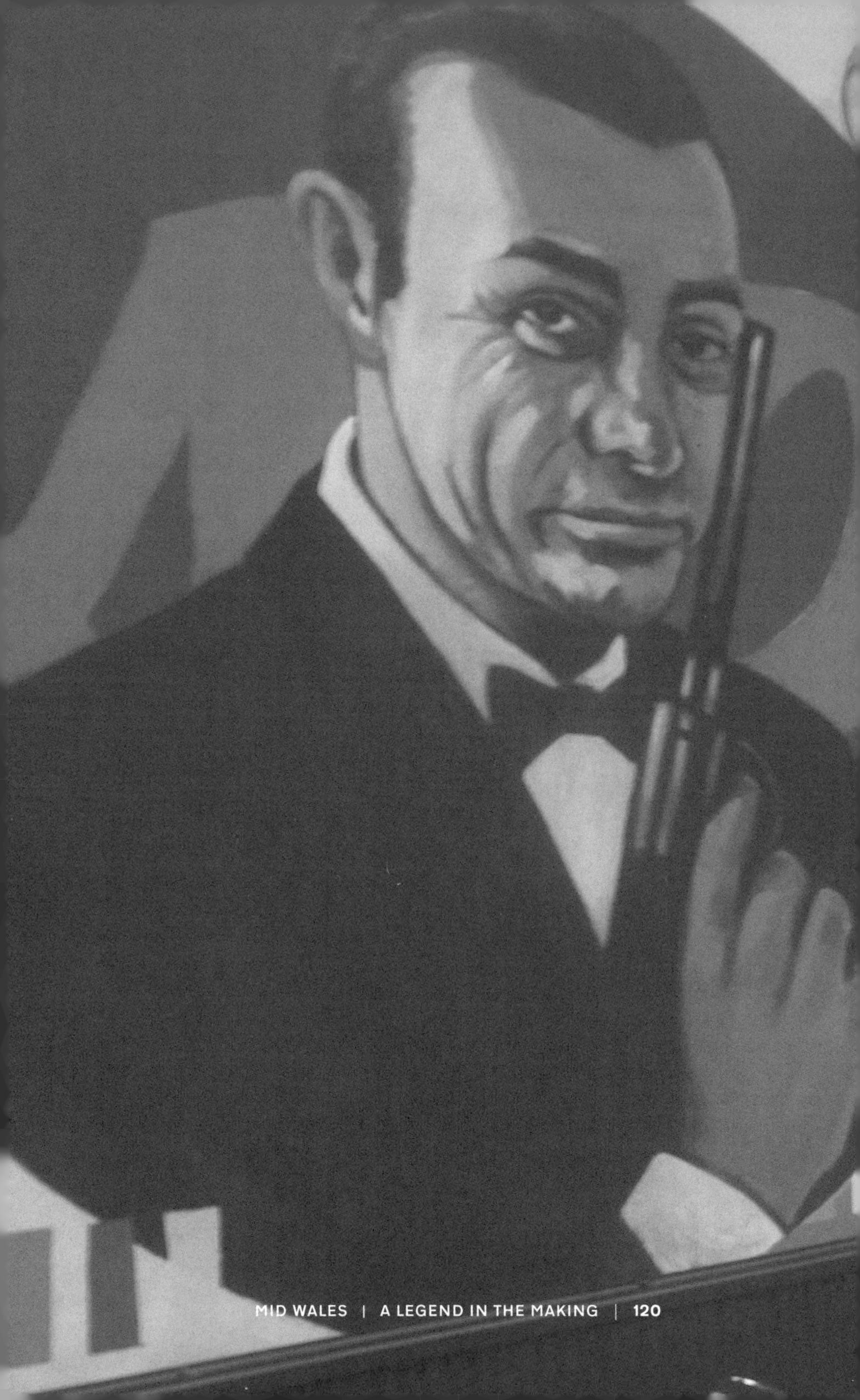

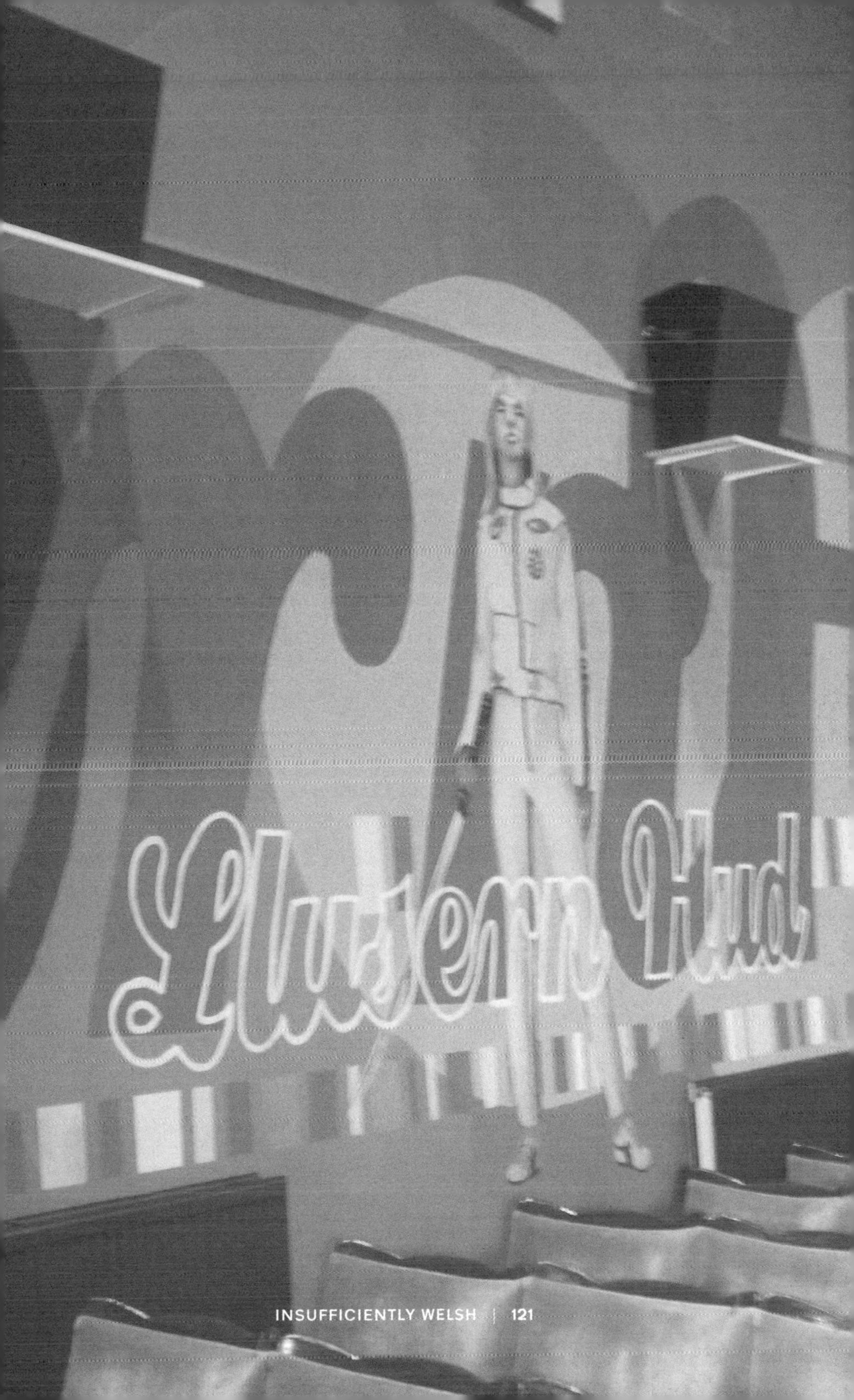
Llusern Hud

"Mid Wales" is not much of a name for a region, is it? Who thought that up? It sounds a bit dismissive. "Middle England" is a non-specific backwater of leather pouffes and yappy terriers; mid Wales seems to promise a conventional flatland, riven with cul-de-sacs and rampant with Nigels, but, far from it, mid Wales is gorgeous. It's a mountainous fairyland. No, really. And I started my trip there in a tree house.

Geographically, mid Wales lies below Snowdonia, on that long, long curving bay that separates the craggy bits of the north and the indented bits of the west. It isn't the furthest to the west and it isn't the hilliest of country, but it is a long way from a direct motorway link. Swathed in forest and splintered by valleys, mid Wales is a place of legend and folklore. This is the Cymru outback – remote Britain (if one slightly colonised by Brummies). It is a separate country. Many claim that Machynlleth is the ancient capital of Wales. It was the seat of Owain Glyndwr's first Welsh parliament in 1404.

An Anglesey resident told me that he once decided to try to get down south by the direct route along the coast. He was frustrated by the distances he had to cover and the lifetime that it had taken him. Nothing speeds your way around mid Wales except recklessness. But when I had finished my assignment here, I turned to drive to Manchester myself, taking a road from Machynlleth up the Dyfi. It was a long tortuous route but as I snaked through the valleys, between the glowing hills, towards Welshpool and Oswestry, I kept wanting to stop and absorb this place: imprint it. I never wanted to relinquish the moment and the landscape.

But that was all to come. For the moment I was standing here wondering why exiles made their way to this coast. What were they looking for? A slower and leafier environment? Something quirky? Perhaps something like the impressive tree house, where I began my quest?

It was high up amongst the trees of west Wales, growing in a steep wood. The huts in the branches were reached by a genuine escalier – a wooden, clambering ladder to the stars. The platform or deck, on which my tubular sleeping pod perched, was 20 to 30 feet up in the canopy. I really needed some excited small kids to enjoy it. We didn't have any, so we played at being kids ourselves.

I needed to get hold of my Mid-Welsh challenge. I wanted

romance. I decided on a Robin Hood postal delivery. It would be cool if it twanged into the pine tree next to me; a message tied to an arrow. The team was worried. The arrow would skewer me. They brought a pulchritudinous Hunger Games archer. (This is not a fantasy-fantasy. She was Diana in a Parka, though called Emily.) She stood just by the camera, pulled back her bow and prepared to fire the arrow straight into the trunk next to me from four feet away. I would cower in the hut, deftly emerge and yank off the message, just like Robin Hood – or Keith Allen anyway.

Tudor set up the camera. He pressed a button and retired. Emily, the huntress, pulled back her aluminium bow and, with a "twong", not a "twang" (it is a base note), the arrow flew at the pine tree and bounced straight back out. There was a pained, metallic clank and it banged around the place before falling to the floor, broken in two.

We concluded that this was highly dangerous. So we tried again. It still didn't skewer the tree, so we ended up writing the challenge on loo paper and I read it off the toilet roll. It wasn't quite the same romantic scenario, but was better from the risk assessment point of view.

My challenge was "to find the Holy Grail".

## – HOLY GRAILS! –

Is there anything particularly Welsh about that fabulous relic, the Holy Grail? As an object, it sounds a little idolatrous. We were in good chapel country here. No room for magic rituals or Papist superstition please, but King Arthur was definitely Welsh and he took this fabulous relic extremely seriously.

There are chauvinistic English claims to the Lord of Camelot. Tintagel tends to feature. There are French King Arthurs too. Probably Breton. (My granny used to say that the Bretons arrived on bicycles in the valleys to sell onions, and they and the Welsh ladies would chatter away to each other. My father used to say they chattered away, but none of them understood a word the other was saying.) The French, however, had a meeting of all their Arthurian historians in Rennes in 2008 and they decided that King Arthur, if he existed at all, was probably Welsh. The first references to him emerge in Welsh myth and poetry in the seventh century and from the eleventh century the stories of his chivalry and valour start to spread across Europe.

King Arthur was an ancient Briton; one of the original race left after the Romans departed, banished to the west by the arrival of the Saxons. He sleeps in a cave in Snowdonia (in case you were wondering) surrounded by heaps of gold, some of which an adventurous local farmer stole until, as always happens in these stories, he became too greedy and got turned into a toad. Arthur lies there still surrounded by his knights, gently napping until called upon to defend the cause of Wales.

This much I knew already. I also knew that many brave knights and fair lords had tried to get the Holy Grail and, er, perished. Lancelot himself had been a little too raunchy to be allowed to have it, Sir Gawain a little too forgetful. (He neglected to pack it in his bags while leaving the thicket.) You needed to be pure of heart to get hold of the Grail. Would I conform? I think so. You may have formed your own opinion, of course.

King Arthur's cave, however, was hidden somewhere up north on the slopes of Snowdon, I was much further down the coast. I would have to look for other grail stories and new Arthurian legends in mid Wales.

## – GOLD FINGERS AND THUMBS –

Gold has a strong association with the region. They have been digging for precious metals in this area of Britain since 1000 BC and the Romans made their way here partly in order to establish a proper mining business. I joined Ben, who drove me to the Clogau site in Bontddu, which in its time had been the most productive of seams in the Dolgellau region, in his Porsche. It had been a very proper mining affair. They had mined for copper and a little lead, and had discovered gold there in 1852, initiating a mini gold rush and extracting about two and a half tons of the yellow stuff before the 1920s. At its peak it was Britain's largest and richest gold mine. But, as Ben told me ruefully, a gold mine is not really "a gold mine". In 2007 it was decided that every scrap of gold that could be extracted had been extracted. They even filtered the road we were walking along.

We were making a steady climb through mature forest along the sides of a rushing river. As we slopped past thundering waterfalls and under massive beeches, Ben explained that there was still a huge worldwide demand for Welsh gold. The Japanese like to get married with a ring made of the slightly tawny metal. It was red because of the amount of copper naturally mixed in to it. The Royal Family wore Welsh gold, not merely for patriotic reasons but because a canny, previous owner of the mines, had delivered a large free nugget into their safe keeping. Their Majesties have about a kilo left, to provide the family with matching gold keepsakes into the foreseeable future. Welsh gold has been worn by their royal highnesses, from Diana, Princess of Wales, to the Queen herself. Kate Middleton's wedding ring was made from the precious metal. Because Welsh gold is so rare, only a bit of the metal is used in high street products which is why legally they have to describe the rings as a "touch of rare Welsh gold" and not "Welsh gold".

Meanwhile I got excited about the shapes I was seeing in the woods. At first, I thought it was an illusion. Perhaps that vast stone wall was just a cliff? But the forest to either side was indeed dotted with grey, lichened ruins: the former engine sheds, furnaces or sleeping quarters of ancient workings.

Ore is dug out and then washed to get at the metal. So the river was important to the process. Trees had naturalised some of the oldest workings. It was as if we were passing a Mayan outpost in the jungle. Suddenly, however, we found ourselves coming to more modern detritus: big blue corrugated iron sheds, rusting containers and rolls of cable. And away, in an insignificant corner, Ben showed me the entrance to the mine itself: a modest four foot high burrow in a low cliff, with a barred metal gate blocking the way forward. We could only peer a few yards into the tunnel, but Ben told me there were a further eight miles of shafts and levels under the mountain.

But the gold was finished. There was no more. Ironically, the ore had been usefully productive. It delivered about thirty troy ounces per long ton. This compares well with South African mines, which can only manage a quarter of a troy ounce per ton. But the South African mines are far more extensive. The comparatively small Welsh seams appear to be all worked out.

Ben wanted to show me how it all began. He was carrying a plastic pan the size of a dinner plate. We could search for gold in the stream. Officially, we needed a permit to do such a thing. You can't just start panning for gold like some grizzled forty-niner, you need a licence to do it. But he offered to show me how, as long as we threw any precious and hugely valuable nuggets back.

We crouched by the water's edge and scooped up some black grit. My pan was corrugated, descending in inverted ziggurat levels, so that as I washed the dirt away the heavier gold could gradually tumble to the bottom. As if. We washed and sifted and jiggled the stuff a bit so the camera might get some idea of the method.

"And what is that?" I asked, casually pointing to a bright fleck in the bottom of the pan.

"Oh that is the gold," said Ben.

"How do you mean?" I asked. "Is that stuff you put in there?" Ben was carrying a little tube of gold flakes, and I thought he might well have set up the pan for the camera.

"No, no," Ben laughed. "The river is full of gold." It was impossible for the process to capture everything, so quite a lot got washed down in the river with the ore.

I looked again more closely. I had imagined we might find something after a long period of sifting, but here was a fleck the first time out. I had swept away the vast majority of the muck I had picked up and, hardly concentrating, because we were chatting for the benefit of the camera, I had reduced my grit to a mere smear in the bottom of my pan.

Now I bent down and looked at the yellow dot as closely as I could. It was minute. It stood out because it shone. Even that miniscule fragment of gold had a distinct lustre in the water at the bottom of my plastic bucket. Suddenly the lure of gold fever gripped me. I could imagine what it was like for a prospector. There was something distinctive about the teeny flake. It seemed to glow. If I stuck my little finger in, I could just about get it to adhere to the tip, but then I could see what a useless amount it was. I leant down, like a proper unlicensed experimenter, stuck my pan in the water and let my gold speck wash away.

If the price goes up any more, I may be back.

## – A MAGIC LANTERN –

I wanted to meet the modern wizard of Aberdyfi: the contemporary myth-maker Geoff Roustabout. This man (formerly Geoff Hill) had recently stepped up to keep Aberdyfi in its seaside wet afternoon entertainment by buying the Magic Lantern Cinema.

Geoff was not much of film buff himself. "Before I owned this place I only went to the cinema four times over ten years," he told me.

Now it took up 30 hours of his time a week. He hated to see "a cultural service" die and he had refurbished the little Welsh seaside resort with its own Greatest Show on Earth: a stylish foyer and a grand auditorium, decorated with impressive murals of the masters of cinema. I hadn't expected to find an art house in the far west. But then when you are remote you have to make your own entertainment.

"We had the full version of 'Lawrence of Arabia' including the interval just the other night," Geoff said proudly, as we settled into his plush tip-up seats. He also showed first-run Hollywood blockbusters and linked up to a network of simulcasts of theatre and opera events.

Geoff was not a local. "I have a tent business," he told me as we watched a film of the local area together. "We make tents for festivals and you'll find our marquees at all the major outdoor events. In fact, my boys are bringing some of the big ones back from Glastonbury even as we speak."

I sensed that Geoff was a proud showman of the old school. He had been in the events business for thirty years and owned his own company for twenty. The same spirit that said "of course we can have a festival for twenty thousand people in these fields" had started to add little extras to Aberdyfi life.

He told me that he had thought about the cinema for a whole weekend. Viewed it on the Friday and bought it on the Tuesday. He had also been influential in the rented tree house holiday villas I had just left.

"Absurdly fantastic things," I ventured.

"All the better for that." Geoff extolled the virtue of enterprise out here in the sticks. People worked harder for less money. They were prepared to try out new ideas. There was little competition.

Geoff had also bought a disused boat yard. "It wasn't expensive," he told me. He had built a clubhouse on his boatyard site by dragging an old fishing boat up on the hard and cutting a door in it. He was currently heavily involved in the attempt to hold onto the Shed of the Year award. He won in 2012 by erecting a shed on a floating pontoon and mooring it just offshore.

That shed had now gone up a nearby mountain to be a "summit shed". The pontoon was put to another use. Geoff took me to his blue BMW sports car. His excited black Labrador climbed on to the back shelf and slid around somewhere between my ears and the plastic rear window (heavily repaired with yellow duct tape) while we swung out, drove through Aberdyfi and followed the shoreline of the estuary alongside the branch railway, towards his base up the estuary.

As we arrived at his slightly overgrown lot, a banana-shaped, 20-foot high grey tower in the parking bay started to whistle and dribble.

"We built it to take around festivals." Geoff explained. "It's steamdriven." It hit the hour. The upper portion telescoped upwards, to reveal a carousel of wooden fish that gyrated around in a cloud of steam. It was a clock.

"The main reason I have settled here," Geoff explained as we walked towards the water under a railway line tunnel, "is because I don't think there is a more beautiful place to be in the world. If I was going to be anywhere and I could be anywhere this was going to be it by choice."

He stopped before the pebbles got slippery, at the tide's edge, adjusted his broad-brimmed fedora, and pointed ahead. "There you are." About 50 yards off the shore a children's trampoline, very like the one at home in the garden for the kids, was leaning slightly askew on top of a floating box.

"Is it safe?"

"I have no idea. It floats. It looks secure. Are you?"

Mark, one of Geoff's helpers, rowed me out. It was indeed secure. The trampoline was firmly anchored to its pontoon. The green padded protection had come unstuck and was flopping about uselessly in a slight chop. But the water around looked cold and unsympathetic. Had the sun been out or had I been an energetic teenager with balls, then the temptation to boing upwards and outwards and attempt a full forward spring-assisted somersault into the Dyfi estuary might have been overwhelming.

I knew that Tudor and Chris were sitting watching carefully and recording every moment. I knew they were hoping that when I bounced the thing would rock and I would lurch forwards fully clothed into the sea for a YouTube classic. But you know… It was nearly lunchtime. I was some way beyond faking incompetence for telly, and the unpadded edges of the trampoline looked sharp and painful. I went up and down. I reached an impressive height. But the contraption was stable enough. I was perfectly in control. That was it. So they all buggered off and marooned me there instead.

## – THE BELLS, THE BELLS –

No doubt Geoff would have been happy to hold an Arthurian hot air balloon tournament in the Tarren Hills, but he knew nothing about the Holy Grail and mid Wales. He admitted, however, that this was a region where people talked about 500 years ago as if it was only yesterday. Almost any strangely shaped rock was likely to accrue a story. There was, for example, a "Bearded Lake" above the town, where King Arthur battled a monster called Afangc, and a rock there was supposed to have a print of his horse's hoof embedded in it. But I needed to get south. I vaguely remembered a story about a big house near Aberystwyth. The details were misty. But it involved lost treasure and holy rituals.

The water in front of Geoff's boatyard runs into a wide, sandy silted-up gulf called the Dyfi Estuary, once used as a location for the 1976 Led Zeppelin film, *The Song Remains The Same*. It was ten miles back to the bridge near Machynlleth. I was looking for a way across. Historically, it was unlikely that I was the first person to face this dilemma. The weekly town market in Machynlleth dates back to 1291, when people from all around the area would have trekked across the estuary to get into town.

Not far from Aberdyfi in Tywyn you'll find Cadfan's stone, which is said by some to be the oldest known written Welsh in existence. Some academics argue that it's the most important object in Welsh history. It's somewhat surprising, then, to find that Tywyn is a very anglicised place, with just over half of its population being born in England. The town has an extremely mixed identity. The Welsh dialect used in this area has its own distinctive features, so much so that one Victorian observer said that there were three languages spoken in the town: English, Welsh and "Tywynacg".

Aberdyfi (or the Mouth of the Dovey) Itself lies on a byway. In World War Two it was home to a secret commando unit of troops from Austria and Germany, trained for espionage missions against the Nazis. These troops became valuable members of the community, with several of them marrying local girls. Now a few seaside cafés were scattered along a quiet front. Buckets and spades, gummy sandals and postcards in wire racks sat like forlorn reminders of simple holidays. It was quiet. There was no sign of any of this legendary activity. I ordered a half a pint of espresso and wandered out to the shore.

I had been promised a lift in a motorised rib. It was going to pick me up on the long spit of sand that ran out to the west beyond the sailing club. But for a while I lingered on the quay, built by the Aberdyfi and Waterford Steam Company in 1887 to import livestock from Ireland.

The sun was low and bright. There were kids jumping into the water (the same freezing water I had so scrupulously avoided earlier), and just beyond them was a hole in the top of the jetty. It commemorated another legend.

I was on the borders of Cantre'r Gwaelod, a Welsh Atlantis that once reputedly stretched 20 miles out into Cardigan Bay. One acre of that rich, fertile, low-lying mythical land was said to be worth four of ordinary grazing. It was drained by a gate in a dyke and protected by shutting the gate to prevent the sea coming back in. But, around AD 600 (and I like the niceness of the date: it brings the myth closer to recorded history) the gatekeeper Seithennin went to a party near Aberystwyth. He got drunk and he forgot his duties. A big storm and a spring tide came blustering in and 16 villages were swamped. And, as with most drowned land legends, on a stormy night they say that the bells can still be heard, swinging in the submerged steeples.

They can certainly be heard today, because the hole in the jetty contains a sea-bell, hanging just beneath the quay, with a clapper attached to a vane that dangles in the water. It keeps the legend alive. As the tide comes in and the wind gets up, so the waves knock against the flat metal flap and a dolorous sound echoes through the village. I listened and I waited. It was high tide, but the sea was calm and the sky was blue. Shrieking children were jumping in the water. The bell stayed obstinately lifeless.

We persuaded one of the boys, however, to swim around and rattle our clapper. He did so and our television viewers enjoyed both a lovely evening half-light and the legendary storm bell donging its clapper. Is that cheating? Probably. So go on, expose us to the papers. We don't care.

## – PETRIFIED FOREST, BRAVE PRESENTER –

Leaving the estuary and striking south, Cardigan Bay became a long ellipse of washed sand in front of an unexpectedly flat plain.

Near Borth, a sea wall prevents breakers overwhelming a straggle of grey houses and bleak shop fronts. They are currently spending 12 million repairing these sea defences. It seemed rather empty, although in 2011 Borth was named one of the top 20 best places for families to live in England and Wales; it was the only one in Wales to make the list. Perhaps they like it empty.

We passed the corpse of a porpoise. It must have washed up on the beach and been put on the new wall to be disposed of. A grey inner tube, slightly swollen, with its eyes pecked out by gulls, it had wholly disappeared by the time we came back, though nobody else seemed to be

about on this windy afternoon. Pity. The Ynyslas sand dunes nearby are
a popular tourist attraction, particularly amongst kitesurfers. The dunes
attract around 250,000 people each year. It was a fine day to be out on
such a wide, uncompromising beach. But it was deserted.

As I strolled along, I saw what I assumed were the remains of a
wreck up ahead. And getting closer I could see the worn ends of wooden
posts, smoothed by the sand. But these were not old boat frames, because
these protrusions had roots.

I crouched down. The stumps of trees were joined to the sand by a
complex and interwoven network, scrambling over and through each itself.
Close to, I could see that the tide had worked like a sander, scouring and
smoothing the wood, and revealing the grain of the original tree. The sand
at the roots gave way to a black, sticky mud-like substance. This was peat.
It was this organic residue that had preserved them. It had an acidic effect
that protected the trees from the natural processes of rot.

I was looking at the remains of trees that grew here some 1,500
years ago. Further to the north, radio carbon dating has identified a
submerged forest that was 2,000 years older still.

It is known that human beings walked amongst these trees,
because perfectly preserved footprints have been found in the peat further
to the north. But it was interesting that the age of this forest near Borth
corresponded to the supposed date of the inundation of Cantre'r Gwaelod,
the Welsh Atlantis. Over the last 2000 years the sea level has varied
considerably. It is generally supposed to have been higher in the Roman
Era. But here was straightforward evidence of a whole forest overwhelmed
by climate change; and without the help of global warming.

These inundations were all happening around the same time that
a supposedly factual Arthur was ruling over Britain. Legend and history
were closing on each other.

## – ABERYSTWYTH –

I am always happy to linger in the "Biarritz of Wales". Aberystwyth is
uncompromisingly "seaside". A granite promenade runs in a magnificent
curve along the front and stands as a bulwark against the Irish Sea. Behind
it, as if staring down the sun, is a terrace of hotels and bed and breakfasts.

It also has a link to the Holy Grail, albeit a rather tenuous one.

Former Aberystwyth mayor Sue Jones-Davies played Judith Iscariot in Monty Python's *Life of Brian*. When it was first released, however, it was banned in the town (the film was banned in a number of places). When Sue Jones-Davies became mayor she sought to rectify this and did so, successfully. Confusingly, it has also since been proven that the ban itself was an urban myth. It didn't happen. Hm. So she overturned something that had not taken place. "Pythonesque!" (as we used to exclaim about anything baffling).

If you leave the front and sneak up any of the backstreets, past the occasional startlingly coloured house, you find yourself in a kindly amalgam of cafés, bike and bookshops. This is a university town. And it has been since 1872. The population varies seasonally, with the coming and going of around 8000 full-time students. It is a remote town too. The nearest big cities are an hour and forty minutes drive away. The railway reached here in 1869. It was late coming, but remains the best way to arrive.

Some say that this isolation is the reason why you can find almost anything in Aberystwyth if you look. It has to be self-sufficient. Anything? Did that include the Holy Grail, I wondered?

But here were seaside and academia combined: two of my favourite recondite things. Aberystwyth is like Brighton, but neater, smaller and quieter. At one end is the castle, which started falling into ruin in the fourteenth century. At the other is the funicular on Constitution Hill. And you must not miss that. It shows no signs of slowing down. Though if it did, it would stop completely. It creeps up a 50 percent gradient at a mountain goat pace, to an invigorating view down the coast towards Pembrokeshire.

Directly behind the town is another hill, and halfway up that is another reason for visiting Aberystwyth: the National Library of Wales. There are treasures enough in the Library itself, which houses over 6,000,000 books, including a manuscript edition of Chaucer, which I had held in my own trembling hands on a previous visit. There are 118 miles of shelving – enough shelving to get you nearly as far as Birmingham by car. The stock of the library grows by around 80,000 each year because of copyright law, which entitles the library to receive a copy of every new book published in the UK. But as the Second World War approached, the institution became even richer when some of the greatest collections in Britain began to send their own treasures to Wales for safety.

I had heard of this before. In fact someone once suggested that we make a programme about it. This is how legends start, of course. I had imagined caverns in a salt mine high in the Cambrian Mountains with vast collections of statues protected from Goering, whose fevered brain was already imagining the Parthenon marbles in his bathroom. But the truth was more prosaic. They went in a specially dug hole under the library.

The miners of south Wales originally organised a subscription of one shilling per man to build the library, inspired by the motto "All knowledge is a privilege". An aerial photograph shows the building that houses the National Library of Wales, designed in 1909 and finished in 1916, sitting squat, square and massive in a great block to the north of the town.

The pedestrian, however, approaches by hundreds of steps. There is one staircase that runs up through trees just off a by-road at the back of the town. Lots of library researchers use it. I know this, because I wanted to take a pee behind one of the trees that shade its route, but it proved almost impossible.

I needed to be comfortable before I entered these extensive, man-made treasure caves. In order to avoid the Blitz, 25 cases were transported from the British Museum alone. The fears were not only genuine but apposite. It is said that the stairs of a Berlin museum ran with melted Trojan gold when the Russians and Allies bombarded. (Another legend. The Schliemann treasures were simply looted.) But drawings by Leonardo Da Vinci, the Magna Carta itself, the works of Chaucer and autograph works from Shakespeare joined paintings by Turner, Michelangelo and Rembrandt in the vaults. And it wasn't just from London: Corpus Christi College was one of the first places to assign stuff. Ten other institutions joined in. I had to hope that my bladder would hold out. Two guys from the library staff wielding electric drills took down the boards that guarded the entrance and I walked in.

In World War One, a quarry in Blaenau Ffestiniog was used to house artwork from the Tate and the National Galleries, including paintings by Van Gogh. It's even rumoured that the crown jewels were stored there. The tunnel I entered in Aberystwyth was little more than head height. A number of rusty-looking steel doors hung ajar. It was supposed to be sealed, but there was graffiti on the walls. Someone had scrawled "Death" on the civil service issue magnolia paint just inside the entrance.

I lit a torch and stepped cautiously inside. The corridor curved away. I followed it, my beam illuminating badly-drawn skulls. The space continued to curve, unvaryingly, except for another bulkhead. I walked on, perhaps no more than a further 20 paces and found myself back at the entrance. That was it. The great treasure cave amounted to less than 100 feet of close tunnel.

It was a little disappointing. I wondered if it had been to the curators and librarians who commissioned it. The absolutely priceless, the really unique and timeless treasures of Great Britain, including letters from Sir Walter Raleigh and Francis Drake, could all be stored in a semi-circular basement no bigger than a couple of containers.

The treasures survived and were disbursed again. I have heard that the Luftwaffe had no strategic interest in the area, though I wasn't aware that the Germans flew such long sorties over west Wales. I have also heard that the RAF used the library as a marker for their own bombers, heading off into the Atlantic, and that had further protected the treasure. This all sounded like embryonic myth-making to me. The embroidery starts. The sheer banality of the cave and its limited dimensions and a few crates and civil service dockets are not enough to satisfy the need for a good myth.

## – NANTEOS –

I used the bookshops and cafés in Aberystwyth to try to get closer to the Legend of the Grail. My faint recollection was correct. The miraculous cup was, indeed, reputed to have been kept at a house a few miles from Aberystwyth, called Nanteos. I hired a bike and pedalled into the suburbs.

Nanteos sits in the wooded Paith Valley. It is a big, cuboid, Grade I-listed block of Georgian mansion, built by William Powell between 1738 and 1757, with money obtained from marriage to a former Lord Mayor of London. It was only recently sold by the Powell family after centuries of private occupation and has become a country hotel. It has 69 rooms, including a highly decorated music room on the first floor where plaster musical instruments are entwined with plaster representations of the four seasons in a plaster fantasy that looks good enough to eat. The house is so big that during winter the second floor used to be closed off to conserve heat. In the 1920s ten members of staff maintained the exterior of the estate alone. Wagner is reputed to have come to call and, as we all know, Wagner wrote "Parsifal". Perhaps he took inspiration from the Holy Grail at Nanteos? Already febrile minds are beginning to see connections. Mine certainly was. The cup that Nanteos sheltered did definitely exist. Whether Wagner saw it is doubtful.

I bounced up a long private drive that comes off a secluded by-road beginning at the very roundabout that marks the entrance to

# ABERYSTWYTH GENERAL

ABERYSTWYTH IS HOME TO THE LONGEST
ELECTRIC CLIFF RAILWAY IN BRITAIN.

THE FIRST INDEPENDENT WELSH EVANGELICAL
CHURCH WAS ESTABLISHED IN ABERYSTWYTH.

IN 1964 THE COLLEGE OF LIBRARIANSHIP
WALES OPENED. AT THE TIME IT BECAME
THE LARGEST LIBRARIAN-TRAINING
INSTITUTE IN EUROPE.

SOME OF THE GREATEST HISTORICAL
ARTEFACTS AND TREASURES IN THE WORLD
WERE REMOVED FROM THE DANGERS OF THE
LONDON BLITZ AND TRANSPORTED TO CAVES
IN ABERYSTWYTH FOR SAFEKEEPING.
THE WORKS INCLUDED: DRAWINGS BY DA VINCI,
THE MAGNA CARTA, WORKS OF CHAUCER,
AUTOGRAPHS FROM SHAKESPEARE, PAINTINGS
OF JMW TURNER, MICHELANGELO AND
REMBRANDT AND EVEN LETTERS FROM
THE LIKES OF SIR FRANCIS DRAKE, SIR WALTER
RALEIGH AND OLIVER CROMWELL.

Aberystwth. There were a few cars scattered around the large square of gravel in front of the porticoed entrance where I slewed to a halt. Leaving a dove-grey, stone-flagged hall, the manager Mark Rawlings-Lloyd immediately escorted me on a tour, which included my room for the night.

Having settled me in and given me time to try all the televisions in my giant suite, Mark escorted me to the morning room off the entrance hallway where he showed me a portrait hanging above the fireplace of a grey-haired matron in a sensible blue floral dress called Margaret Powell. She owned Nanteos in the thirties.

We stood in front of the picture, like minor characters in a black-and-white movie, while Mark explained that Mrs Powell and her servants had entertained a stream of sick visitors seeking the grail and its healing properties. They were led through a well-attested and carefully rehearsed ritual and Mark demonstrated it all, complete with movements.

The patient was kept waiting, exactly where I stood, and the cup itself, a wooden bowl made of wych elm, was placed on a small table in the next room. There it was filled with water.

At a given signal (Mark ushered me on), Mrs Powell and the visitor came through to the library via the adjoining door. (We did so.) The supplicant was allowed to drink the water out of the bowl on the small table (I looked at a table), heal themselves or whatever, and was then quickly bundled out. (That was through the door where we had just entered.)

Mark explained that Mrs Powell always slammed the door behind her. This was a cue for her servant to take the real bowl to a secure place and replace it with a fake one; presumably to stop the desperate invalid returning in the middle of the night, with a bag marked "swag". The real thing was locked away. The fake was there as a lure. This was all very thrilling.

This was all organised because the bowl had accrued miraculous properties and everybody seems to have heard about it. The family had kept records dating from 1850. They showed that, in earlier, less paranoid times, the thing had been loaned out on approval, in return for "something of value", sometimes for months on end, and then given back when it had done its duty. These notes detailed its universal medical success. It was better than antibiotics, by the sound of it.

Quite how the miraculous crockery of the Lord was supposed to have worked its way to Nanteos required a considerable blending of myth, story, fantasy and conjecture. As sceptics have tended to point out, the cup had no real significance in any biblical account. Jesus seems to have grabbed what was handy and then left it for the washing up. But Joseph of Arimathea was reputed (an important word in this story) to have used that same bowl to gather the blood of Christ in the tomb. (Several gallons of this blood have subsequently been distributed, usually in gold vials, knobbly with precious stones, to important cathedrals and monasteries.)

It is not difficult to see the symbolism. Here are some of the basic tenets of the Catholic Church combined in a cup, blood and communion. It became a significant vessel in legend. And the legend was that Joseph travelled across the known world to Glastonbury, carrying his cup in his personal baggage. Glastonbury was indeed a Roman outpost. (There are always handy connections with reality in any legend.) He seems to have left his cup in the safekeeping of the garrison. In due course it was handed over to some monks who established a monastery there.

We move forward in time. About 1,000 years later, Henry VIII decided to actively disrupt the contemplative life in Britain. Seven Glastonbury monks fled his desecrations and took the relic to Strata Florida: a Cistercian monastery in the "valley of the flowers" in mid Wales; that too was later dissolved by Henry VIII. Some of the monastery became a country house, and this country house was at one point owned by the Powells. Ahah! Here's the final connection. This was the family that built Nanteos. They became the guardians of the mystic mug.

Tortuous and improbable, but definitely worth hearing, and since I had come so far, I was gullible and excited. "So do you have it now?" I breathed.

Mark was apologetic. "No, the cup was not sold with the contents of the house, I fear. It stayed with the family." He reached over and picked up a framed photograph. It was all he could offer me by way of compensation.

I stared at a grainy black-and-white image of a round, moulded, chewed-up lump of dark wood. The original vessel has been estimated to be 12cm round. This looked a bit smaller. It had lost some of its edges and half the bowl too.

Of course, now I was in another film. I was in *The Maltese Falcon*. I had got close to the craved object, but it wasn't the real thing at all. Like Sydney Greenstreet, I would have to get on my bike and head off to Germany or somewhere, to pursue it further in a relentless, never-ending deadly quest.

Since it clearly wasn't the Holy Grail, I couldn't be bothered. There are several other pretenders to holy cupdom, anyway. It has been established that the object I was looking at was most probably a "mazer" cup, from around the thirteenth century: the sort of humble wooden vessel that a monk would have used for lunch.

A significant proportion of the cup had been lost. Some had rotted away, but quite a lot had been broken off deliberately. It was a constant problem with any holy, miraculous relic. If the water drunk from the thing had curative properties, how much more effective might be the thing itself. Well, let's find out. Chomp, chomp, nibble, nibble. Visitors had taken to surreptitiously chewing off a bit of the cup while slurping down its contents. No wonder Margaret Powell had watched over the proceedings so closely.

So I failed in my quest. This was the right area alright. I hadn't touched the Holy Grail. I merely discovered that plenty in the area were convinced that they had. It was another legend that had been sewn into the fabric of this fantasy-weaving region. Gold mines, fairies, sunken bells, lost forests and hidden national treasures; mid Wales was a country that liked stories. It was, thankfully, a lot less prosaic than Middle England, and I was grateful for that.

# SNOWDONIA

## A LILY IN THE VALLEY

SNOWDONIA | A LILY IN A VALLEY | 144

INSUFFICIENTLY WELSH | 145

# – FANTASY PRISON –

Just like you, I know Portmeirion. I had never been there but I'd seen the pictures. I watched *The Prisoner* and was quite disturbed by an oversized inflated beach ball bouncing harmfully after Patrick McGoohan. (I am that old and I was that young.)

I'm not the only one who feels this way either: every year, hoards of *Prisoner* fans flock to Portmeirion for their own festival called 'Festival Number 6'. It's become so popular in the last few years that The Manic Street Preachers joined its 2013 line up. But I never felt obliged to visit. Portmeirion was one of those places that I assumed would disappoint, as fantasies often do.

Of course, that assumed knowledge was a fantasy in itself. I had no idea where the architect Clough Williams-Ellis's renowned creation actually was. The sat nav wasn't much help as we approached Penrhyndeudraeth on the estuary of the River Dwyryd, creeping around largely suburban approaches in the twilight. So we got lost three times, cautiously driving down steep roads, past scattered buildings and through highly decorated, manned gates. I barely understood that the houses were divided up and rented out as hotel rooms. Or that some people return again and again. Or that it was genuinely enchanting.

My car was deposited on the hill. Reception was down by the sea. The porter took me to my accommodation in a golf buggy. I passed through a small garden and into the clock tower. My suite was a pair of comfortable garden rooms with a lot of tiny widows with a lot of tiny curtains to pull that never really cut out the morning light. So I woke at dawn.

I recommend you check in and fail to make the curtains work; it's the only chance you will get to really appreciate the appeal of Portmeirion. I climbed steps, descended alleys, traipsed through gardens, crossed under palm trees, along pergolas, round behind cottages, through arches, past capriccios, along every crazy, jumbled adaptation and architectural invention completely on my own, until I found main reception and my breakfast, which was finally served on a table outside my room, anyway.

By nine o'clock the entire village was crammed. Portmeirion is one of Wales's big attractions, drawing in over 250,000 visitors a year. Not unhappily. It absorbs them, like a proper village *en fête*, rather than an over-visited museum. Despite its obvious stagey qualities, it doesn't

# PORTMEIRION

STAR OF 'THE PRISONER' PATRICK McGOOHAN TURNED DOWN THE ROLE OF JAMES BOND.

THE SCRIPTWRITER BEHIND THE SERIES, GEORGE MARKSTEIN, LEFT THE PROJECT AFTER 13 EPISODES WHEN HE CLASHED WITH McGOOHAN ABOUT HOW THE SERIES SHOULD END. MARKSTEIN FAVOURED A MORE CONVENTIONAL ENDING.

THE PORT PART COMES BECAUSE OF THE AREAS POSITION ON THE COASTLINE, WHILE 'MEIRION' DERIVES FROM THE FORMER NAME OF THE LOCAL REGION 'MEIRIONNYDD'.

AS WELL AS BEING A RENOWNED ARCHITECT, CLOUGH WILLIAMS-ELLIS WAS AN ENVIRONMENTAL CAMPAIGNER AND A FOUNDING MEMBER OF THE COUNCIL FOR THE PROTECTION OF RURAL ENGLAND IN 1926 AND THE WELSH EQUIVALENT IN 1928.

THE PORTMEIRION BUDDHA STATUE WAS A PROP LEFT BEHIND FROM THE INGRID BERGMAN FILM 'INN OF THE SIXTH HAPPINESS'.

SIR CLOUGH WILLIAMS-ELLIS DIED IN APRIL 1978, AGED 94. IN ACCORDANCE WITH HIS WISHES, HE WAS CREMATED, AND HIS ASHES WENT TO MAKE UP A MARINE ROCKET, WHICH WAS PART OF A NEW YEAR'S EVE FIREWORK DISPLAY OVER THE ESTUARY AT PORTMEIRION SOME TWENTY YEARS AFTER HIS DEATH.

feel like a Walt Disney creation. It has a bolt-on eccentricity. One rescued building or invented facade followed another between 1925 and 1975. Clough Williams-Ellis carried on tinkering with his mock Italian paradise until his death aged 94. The main aesthetic is one of glorious and thoughtful improvisation. But it is also, essentially, a garden.

I met Gwynedd by the border under the long brick wall. He and his team were spreading chocolate-coloured bark chippings under ivy-green dark-red standard roses.

I was surprised, as some of you might be, that he was called Gwynedd. My mother is called Gwynneth. Um, I thought Gwynedd was a girl's name. This was not something I felt I could suggest to Gwynedd himself, who was genetically about six foot four and built like a prop forward, but I did anyway and he happily explained that it was gender neutral. (The female version tends to be 'Gwyneth' while the male is 'Gwynedd'.) Possibly confusing on a North Welsh dating site, but yet another cultural test for me.

Gwynedd told me that the "Snowdon Lily", my quest for the day, was not an outward-bound soprano, but a hardy little Alpine. I understood that "Alpines" grow in crevices in suburban bungalows in parts of Buckinghamshire, but the Snowdon Lily needs a specific environment. Mountainous terrain makes a speciality of developing microclimates. It is not simply that as you go higher, different temperatures encourage different growth. Let us imagine a deep gully. The sun may shine directly onto one side, but seldom hit the other. It may experience limited rainfall. Ice may take longer to melt. There might be a specific type of acidic rock. All these factors encourage very specific fauna to adapt to microclimates. I could see why I was being challenged to find one. They wanted me to go up that mountain again.

## – SNOWDONOMANIA –

Snowdon is a magnificent Welsh protruberance and, as we all know, the highest mountain in the whole of the Principality. In consequence, everybody who arrives north of Bala feels obliged to get up it. Perhaps it's because Edmund Hillary used Snowdon as a base camp for training before tackling Everest.

Sitting at the bottom one Saturday morning, some ten years ago,

I was struck by the strange magnetism of the word "highest". A morning rush hour, clad in pastel Gore-Tex, was assembling to "conquer the peak". They could have taken a train (had they walked around the other side, been lazier and braved the queues). At the top, they would find it was a question of waiting in line to mount the summit, to note the improperly dispersed human ashes (it is a prime spot for a bit of scattering), before lamenting the cloud cover and having a nice cup of tea in the new restaurant. I hear Everest has similar problems, though at Eryri you are less likely to die in base camp.

At that time I had been impressed by how the majority of the Saturday climbers were in sturdy boots and sensible socks. Over 350,000 visitors reach the summit each year. These were not casual trippers like the beer boys and wedding parties on Ben Nevis. They had taken precautions by visiting Blacks. How can you not salute the family that clambers together. Ever since the Romantic poets followed in the pony-tracks of Thomas Pennant, at the end of the eighteenth century, so the public has got itself up onto the roof of Wales. A particularly sharp drop is known as Cwm Hetiau, the "valley of the hats", because headgear blew off in the train's slipstream and the locals made money ransoming it at the bottom. It is about 2,000 feet up. Snowdon is now part of the history of tourism. Nobody even wears hats any more. And the carriages are now enclosed. The whole experience is as much about tradition as exertion.

All this seemed to tell me that the Snowdon Lily is a remarkable survival. It clings on despite the march of thousands. I would find it on the flank of Yr Wyddfa, the Tomb, the great mountain itself. My challenge meant I had to put aside all thoughts of Tryfan and Glyder Fawr and other, less-trodden hills and join the mob on the universal common-as-muck mountain trek.

In fact the mob was getting a bit much in Portmeirion. It was time to be moving on, but before I did, Gwynedd took me off to show me a little-regarded corner of his kingdom.

There is a U-bend in the approach road to Portmeirion. I had passed it myself the night before. Now we stood and peered over a low wall that stopped buggies falling to their doom.

A little spring emerged from the cliff. It was typical of what really makes Portmeirion intriguing. I realised that here was lush and very careful planting, in a quiet, almost forgotten corner. Gunnera and bog plants and glossy ferns were growing under a canopy of tall beeches. Gwynedd looked after these woodland perennials with as much attention as the parterres in

# GENERAL SNOWDON

MORE THAN 26,000 PEOPLE LIVE
WITHIN SNOWDON NATIONAL PARK.

---

SOME SAY THE NAME SNOWDON COMES
FROM THE OLD ENGLISH FOR 'SNOW HILL',
OTHERS SAY IT'S BECAUSE WHEN SAILORS
WENT BY IT ON THE COAST, THE MOUNTAIN
IN THE DISTANCE LOOKED LIKE 'SAND DUNES'
OF SNOW, 'SNOW DUNES'. THE WELSH NAME
'YR WYDDFA' MAY HAVE MEANT 'TOMB' OR
'MONUMENT' AND IS MOST LIKELY A REFERENCE
TO A LEGEND OF A GIANT BEING BURIED ON
THE MOUNTAIN.

---

SNOWDON IS THE HIGHEST MOUNTAIN
IN WALES AT 3,560FT.

---

ACCORDING TO WELSH FOLKLORE, THE GIANT,
RHITTA GAWR, IS BURIED ON THE SUMMIT
OF SNOWDON. RHITTA GAWR WAS KILLED
BY KING ARTHUR.

the village centre. And he pointed to what he wanted me to see. It was a Chinese Lily, not yet in flower, but stately and green and rare, poking up through the rocks. It bore the mark of true eccentricity. Portmeirion is not really about display, it is about completeness. Magnificent as it was, however, Gwynedd's five foot green stalk certainly wasn't a weeny Snowdon Lily. That would have to come later.

## – BOATS AND DAMES AND TRAINS –

Time, as Einstein has pointed out, is relative, particularly to cameramen. It is scientifically curious how a space-time dimension can stretch, but not a filming schedule. Now we were pursued by a tide, and the tide was going out.

The illusion of the little harbour with the quayside and its descending steps and the concrete yacht (possibly the least successful touch in the entire place) was receding. I had been promised a lift in a rowing boat and in a few minutes it would be unable to reach me. So I ran – like a less well-dressed Patrick McGoohan – my red parka tails flapping behind me as I dived across the Italian parterre, down the balustraded steps and jumped into a Celtic longboat.

The women who were carrying me onwards often took part in lengthy rowing races across the Irish Sea or up the Severn. (Shortly after they delivered me, they came first in the Great River Race in London.) Their Celtic longboat held four rowers on fixed seats and a cox in the stern to steer. It was built to cross the high seas and was made of fibreglass. They came from Porthmadog. In fact that's where they were taking me. As we skimmed across the shallow water, just off a green and luscious wooded shore, with the huge expanse of the Dwyryd estuary opening out ahead, I envied them their hobby. This was perfect. Except that I wanted to row. I love rowing. Alas, there wasn't time to put me in the team. I had to crouch in the front, making the boat bow down and difficult to steer. I apologised. But for once I had nothing to do except bask in sun and the beauty.

Disembarking, I bought a ticket for the Blaenau Ffestiniog Railway that links the sea to the sky. Porthmadog itself was an artificial creation: a port large enough to carry slates away to roof Hamburg Cathedral and the floors of Boston airport. It was created to serve the monster industry in the hills.

The railway seems to start in the middle of the town: an open display of steam and hissing engines, surrounded by houses and shops. It is 150 years since the first steam locomotives were installed. Two of the original locomotives are still working and now these petite engines and their small-scale carriages with their perfect Victorian interiors are a tourist attraction. They are not miniature, they are narrow gauge, just a bit more dinky than the average train. They were pioneering locomotives as well. The technology first developed on these lines was exported around the world and showed the doubters that steam locomotives could be cost-effective.

The guard arrived to lock me in, still considered a necessity on this steep track. We chugged off, temporarily crossing flat land by the mole that created the harbour and then, almost immediately, climbing upwards. Originally, the trains of slate coming down had worked entirely by gravity. Brakemen rode on the wagons, jumping from car to car and adjusting levers to control the descent. There were knotted strings dangling from branches to alert them to tunnels.

Boiling 300 gallons of water an hour on the really steep bits, we chuffed up towards the little enclave of industrialisation that Blaenau had once been and which had excluded it, as a doughnut of unsightliness, from the National Park that surrounded it. Except that it was far from unsightly. My eyes were riveted.

The hillsides around the old slate-mining town, once the second largest town in North Wales with a population of 12,000, were a chaos of frenzied pixels of slate. There were slate fences (the plates of the fence anchored to each other by wire), there were slate walls (magnificent irregular black-bricked cross-weaves of slate), there were slate paviours underfoot and slate tiles on the roofs, but the real sight was the wasted slate. It seemed as if the side of every mountain round about had been ripped apart. No doubt tons had been cloven, chipped, smoothed and carried away, but the stuff left behind, the jagged residue, the blocks, shards and wedges of black or grey stone, are piled up in mountainous heaps like frozen black fountains. A slate-working area is a unique industrial landscape, more worthy of a visit than a sheep-shorn hillside. I had an urge to return with a lorry and make sculptures like Richard Long's with some of this residue. Except that these shards are often sculptures in themselves. Collectively they represent a dreadful scarring but a magnificent one. Gradually, so they say, all the waste is being gathered up and ground down to make beds for roads.

As if to make up for its exclusion from the paradise of the National

# PORTHMADOG

TWO HUNDRED YEARS AGO
PORTHMADOG WAS A REGULAR HAUNT
FOR SMUGGLERS.

---

AT ITS PEAK IN 1873, OVER 116,000 TONS
OF BLAENAU SLATE LEFT PORTHMADOG
FOR ALL PARTS OF THE WORLD.

---

PORTHMADOG FOOTBALL CLUB IS ONE
OF THE OLDEST IN WALES AND
WAS FOUNDED IN 1884.

---

LAWRENCE OF ARABIA WAS BORN
JUST OUTSIDE OF PORTHMADOG
IN NEARBY TREMADOG.

---

PORTHMADOG WAS NAMED AFTER
WILLIAM MADOCKS WHO BUILT
A SEA WALL, THE COB, IN 1811 TO
RECLAIM LAND FROM THE SEA

---

POET PERCY BYSSHE SHELLEY STAYED
IN WILLIAM MADOCKS' HOUSE IN TREMADOG
WHEN HE LET IT OUT TO RAISE MONEY FOR
THE COB, AND WROTE QUEEN MAB THERE.

Park, the town had now had its own tourist friendly makeover. Walking up from the station I passed over an ovoid intersection of the road and some stainless steel monoliths erected in memory of the slate workers with a seemingly random 1980s' craft fair aesthetic.

"Do you know how much that costs?" my guide asked me.

I shook my head.

"Four and a half million," he said.

Now he shook his head.

## – ZIP WIRES –

A zip wire is not a new idea at the quarry in Penrhyn. There was one in action when it was a fully operational big hole. ("The biggest manmade hole in the world until 1953," according to my guide.) At that time, it ran across the slate quarry to carry the large blocks of highly compressed mud, which is what slate effectively is, down to the splitters, whose particular skill was to extract a number of slivers of stone out of a single quarried piece.

I've tried it. It requires a knack. I stuck my chisel across the slab, tapped and a tile fell away. Had you roofed your lowly cottage with my slates, though, the rafters would have collapsed. My tile was the width of a chocolate bar. A good splitter could create a dozen, wafer-thin eighteen-inch-square after-dinner mints out of one bit. He bid for the piece he was to work and failure to get his tiles out of it cost him his "profit" (or wages, as his money might more properly have been described). It was a particularly demanding form of piecework.

The slate-quarrying industry seems to have been an exemplar of ruthless industrial exploitation. In Penrhyn, the workers, dying from lung disease and helpless to influence their wages, even after a three-year strike (the longest in British industrial history) at the beginning of the twentieth century, were Welsh and the owners were English. (Or happened to be so. In the equally notorious Lake District, of course, everybody was English.)

Welsh slate was used to re-roof the city of Hamburg after the fire of 1842. It created the familiar grey roof-vista, shining blackly in the wet industrial north of Britain. Welsh slate can also be seen in a number of royal treasures. In Penrhyn Castle you'll find a one-ton slate bed made for Queen Victoria, and in Caernarfon Castle there is the slate stool, designed by Lord Snowdon, used in Prince Charles's investiture. And as we swerved around hairpin bends on a grey wet sludge of a roadway, I was told it was largely health and safety that prevented these quarries remaining competitive. Or perhaps not, because, when we reached the very top of the slate mountain, there were clearly lorries crawling about way below us. In fact, Penrhyn is still the largest single slate quarry in the world, supplying 85 percent of today's Welsh slate. "The working quarry is now to the north," my driver explained. "They still cut the best slate in the world here, but it is expensive to produce."

And now people come to fly over the devastation for fun, like human cannon balls, spat out at speeds of 100 miles an hour at a cost of 50 quid.

## – THE FALL –

"Stand over on the step there with your heels on the lip." I had already been weighed, helmeted and helped into my red Gore-Tex costume. I had pulled a pair of one-piece disposable plastic goggles down over my face. I was a ziponaut, following an established pre-launch routine.

"Now lie down and assume a press-up position." I did so and a part of my protective clothing was wrenched aft and downwards like a tube. "Raise your legs." A bar attached to the front of my jacket was pulled up and under. My feet made contact. "Press your feet backwards." I did so and extended my legs. It stretched me out, as if to tie everything together. Don't do this if you are claustrophobic.

I was now swaddled. I found it comforting. I was in my own papoose - a baby carriage, hooked up to the wire and, having watched others go, I knew that they were now securing a tie line and snap shackle, which simply stopped me slithering away prematurely. And then I hung there for 10 minutes while they set up the camera.

Meanwhile the release master was reading out my details: my weight and disposition. (Number one wire or number two. They stand side by side.) Calculations were constantly being made, concerning the prevailing wind conditions and my likely gravitational pull. I had my weight in kilos – 79 – including boots and costume – inscribed on my wrist in marker pen. Had I been heavier, they would have attached a black or yellow canvas triangle to my back designed to slow my progress, had I been lighter they would have added weights. There is a dip down into the middle of the line. If you go too slowly you can fail to gather enough momentum to fly on up the other side. But everything was one for me. I had no choice in the matter and no identifiable feelings of insecurity either. I had become a package. My arms were free, but the rest of me was trussed like an oven-ready chicken in a scarlet wrapping.

Perfectly balanced, I was simply dangling, face forward, next to a gigantic precipice. I was looking down at a pavement terrace of crushed slate a few feet below me. With a count down of "three, two, one, go!" echoing somewhere on a radio, there was a click above me and I rolled off, not hectically or with any form of stomach-turning acceleration. There was no swoop or lurch, I swept away simply and smoothly with a steady forward motion, immediately picking up alarming speed, and then more speed, and after that more speed again.

The ground below dropped away from my transit, then rose again as we crossed first one terrace and then another, before it suddenly voided out to reveal the poisonous blue of a lake of water in the bowl of the mine below. The slight, misty drizzle stung my face, my mouth filled with inrushing air and my cheeks walloped out, like Wallace and Gromit at speed.

Now I was going at 90 to 100 miles an hour. The mile-long distance to the stopping point was covered in well under a minute. And during those few seconds, I was able to glance about me and note exquisite green countryside. There were hill farms and a village with a church at the very edge of the slate bowl. Twisting to the right, I saw how effectively nature was grabbing the territory back. The old workings were already clothed in trees that the "white woolly maggots" of sheep would never have allowed over the rest of Snowdonia.

It was all gone in an instant. The brown, far side of the pit was rushing up towards me and the galvanised gantries of the other end of the wire were embracing me. There was another click and I slowed. Nothing violent, no sudden jerks, I was just eased into deceleration and a charming girl in mountain gear was holding a metal pole up towards me.

"Take the hook," she said.

I did. More ritual.

She used the hook to stop me rolling back further than she wanted, and my willing suspension was at an end. Now I was instructed to stand. I did.

"Did you enjoy that?" I expect that this was more ritual too. But I had, and I told her so.

# – CHOIR PRACTICE –

I met the boys in the pub in Blaenau and confessed that I was hardly great
choir material. On previous form, I should have been sent down for 10
years' hard practice.

Does the entire Welsh nation sing well? Are they genetically
predisposed to musical capability? My father was a croaker and we took
care to stand a distance from him at wedding services. He gave the lie
to the claim that Welsh people have "great voices". Anyway, it's a minim
away from "what a wonderful sense of rhythm you coloured people have",
isn't it?

I have experienced musical racism myself, and I accuse my mother.
She was convinced I could sing. I was tiny. A Midhurst church throbbing
with a full congregation of envious parenthood is not the place to find
out that you don't quite have command of the piping treble solo in "Once
in Royal David's City". I cracked on the Everest of the treble part – a big
climb in a public place – "Mary was that mother mild". I am breaking out
in hives even now.

I suppose it was my mother's idea that I would look sweet in one
of those cake frills and a red frock marching into Epping Church behind
the incense some three years later. Reader, I was "Welsh", and that meant
one thing in Essex (where we had now moved): I could sing. Two services,
every Sunday, for five years, never proved otherwise.

Then Mr Best pointed a finger at me and condemned me to penal
servitude in the Brentwood School East House Choir. They beat the time
into you. I learned on the gently tapping hoof. I also learned that the best
way to survive was to open your mouth in time with the music and let
nothing at all emerge. Or, at least, until Mr Best started prowling the back
row of the "tenors" and "basses" with an ear cocked.

So I can bellow along with the best of them. I have even sung in a
musical, but all my personal training has been based on the Tony Soprano
model – singing along with major seventies classics while driving too fast.

Mindful of this, I entered the school hall, where fifty members of
the Côr y Brythoniaid were sitting in ranks, restless and murmuring, like a
dozing monster waiting to be poked into life.

John, the choirmaster, was addressing them in Welsh so I settled
in my seat, poised between the baritones and tenors (just for safety)
and honed my look of concerned attention. I would need it if he started
talking music. At least I understood three words of Welsh. I peered at

my score. Yup. I knew which my line was. He pointed it out. I could see the notes going up and down. It's surprisingly helpful. But most of all I listened carefully to the bloke with the 'tache sitting next to me and hoped I could pull off the Tony Soprano trick of singing along a nano-second after everybody else.

Between 1966 and 1974 Côr y Brythoniaid entered 26 competitions and won 19 first prizes. It was founded to bring together a community fracturing with the decline of the slate industry. It became a mighty force in the highly competitive world of battling choirs. We were pretending my visit was a form of audition, but did I really want to pass? They currently faced a demanding schedule of foreign tours and gala appearances in Hungary, with some challenging hotel accommodation thrown in as well, no doubt.

John Eifon was a big chap. Now he drew himself up and, like a magician, or a druid with a powerful spell to weave, which clearly required sheer force of personality, he waved his magic wand and woke the sleeping dragon.

Jan Morris, the celebrated Welsh writer, once commented that if you want to experience the power of a male voice choir, you should attend a rehearsal. I can go one better. Attend and sit in the middle of the singers. A great soaring noise engulfed me. Chocolate, dark, swirling, warm, it lifted the hairs on the back of my neck and surged into the cavity of my chest. They began with a famous Welsh hymn, one so revered and sacred and familiar, that, naturally, I didn't know it at all, but it brought tears to my eyes. And then we sang "Delilah".

Here was a tune for me, straight from the Tom Jones catalogue. I might even have sung along with this belter in the car. This was the moment to let my own voice join the swelling throng. For three glorious minutes I fancied that my tenor chords mingled with this great and lovely noise and helped create a harmonious and stirring version of the sixties power ballad. I opened up the mouth and let rip.

You know the sound that a rip makes, of course. It's a shredding, tearing noise. On the telly you will hear a magnificent harmonious chorale. Later, however, Brian on sound, who had linked me up to an independent microphone, was able to do something that Mr Best in my school choir had never been able to do. He quieted down the rest of the fifty strong choir and allowed my own voice to stand alone.

Oh dear. I had better join my father at the back of the church.

# BLAENAU FFESTINIOG

THE ACTUAL USE OF SLATE IN BUILDINGS
DATES BACK TO THE ROMANS WHEN THEY USED
SLATE IN NORTH WALES CASTLES IN AD 77.

---

BLAENAU FFESTINIOG IS KNOWN AS
'THE TOWN THAT ROOFED THE WORLD'.

---

OAKELEY QUARRY WAS SO LARGE THAT
IT HAD 50 MILES WORTH OF RAILROAD
TRACK UNDERGROUND.

---

AT THE PEAK OF THE WELSH SLATE INDUSTRY
TOWARDS THE END OF THE 19TH CENTURY OVER
HALF A MILLION TONS OF SLATE WAS BEING
PRODUCED EACH YEAR BY A WORKFORCE
NEARING 17,000.

---

THE BLAENAU FFESTINIOG RAILWAY IS
THE OLDEST INDEPENDENT RAILWAY COMPANY
IN THE WORLD

---

DURING WWII SOME OF BRITAIN'S GREATEST
TREASURES WERE STORED IN THE MINES TO
PROTECT THEM FROM BOMBING. ABERYSTWYTH
LIBRARY WAS THE MAIN STORAGE FACILITY BUT THE
MINES HAD WORKS BY RUBENS, REMBRANDT AND
MICHELANGELO. THERE ARE EVEN STORIES THAT THE
CROWN JEWELS WERE KEPT SAFE THERE IN SECRET.

# – A LILY OF THE VALLEY –

Hywel met me at the train station in Llanberis to search for Lloydia
Serotina in the mountains. He was a local reserve manager for the region,
and therefore an expert on the elusive flower, once known as Mountain
Spiderwort. He had himself waited two years before he found a Snowdon
Lily. I was to share his secret tryst.

It felt odd to be setting off to search for an ice age relict of such
rarity by public transport. We were on the early train. It was taking the
staff up to the café on the summit of Snowdon. High winds had been
forecast. There was a feeling of exhilaration in the carriage.

"What happens if it really blows?" I asked.

"We get the day off if the train can't get up there," a boy in a dark
shirt explained. The winds were monitored electronically, as red numbers
on marker boards by the side of the track. Nonetheless, there seemed to
be an element of human judgment involved, because when we lumbered
to a stop, short of the top, there was further debate and a driver and guard
got out and peered up the line as if trying to estimate whether they might
get blown bodily over the cliff. Unlike most trains, the engine on the
Snowdon Mountain Railway actually pushes the train, rather than pulling
it, for safety reasons.

Hywel and I left them at that point and marched off down the
great tourist path towards the Black Cliff, revered by some as the "shrine
of British climbing".

I have to be careful here. You may be more familiar with the
geography of Wales's most populous mountain than I am, so don't look
too hard for clues. This is a secret location. Let's just say we tramped for
a bit along a mountain trail: one of those wide stony thoroughfares that
tourists need and I always think must resemble medieval roads.

Hywel pointed out the exotic natural life like the ravens bouncing
on the hillsides; perhaps relatives of the birds that occupy the Tower of
London, where Brân, the legendary Welsh King of Britain, had his head
buried under the White Tower, according to the Mabinogion.

It was early and hot, but within two minutes we passed our first
semi-unclothed human of advanced age wobbling his pale dugs up
towards us. Then we turned left, followed a path back towards the face of
the mountain and finally started to climb upwards across a steep slope of
scree under a high cliff. As we paused to put on our hard hats, a party of
climbers traversed past us to set up station further to the south. "I always

wear a helmet now," said Hywel. "It's not a difficult climb physically, but there are loose rocks above." Ten years ago, while he had been exploring close to the cliff something had knocked him unconscious.

It was a blazing morning. Historically, the earliest amateur explorers climbed at night in order to catch dawn over the Irish Channel, only to be frustrated by persistent cloud cover. Many met nothing but dense fog. Many still do. But I have never climbed Snowdon (or chugged up it) except on a clear day. Now, on this early June morning, after rain, looking out on the sweep of the mountains and Anglesey beyond, with the sharp blue sea stretching out to the horizon, I once again experienced the glory of Eryri. It's said that on exceptionally clear days from the top of Snowdon you can see Ireland, Scotland, England and the Isle of Man; 24 counties, 29 lakes and 17 islands.

It was a place of blankness and gigantic geometry. Below us, farms sent cultivated fingers probing into the hills, but they reached no further than the bottom of the valley. An improbable swathe of greensward ran in a colossal smooth parabola down and around the side of the hill. With flat black cliffs, no trees, worn-looking escarpments, and a landscape so airbrushed and smooth from a distance, it is peculiar to discover that it is rough and cluttered close up.

The sward is not smooth but uncomfortably bumpy. The slopes are huge, impenetrable walls of boulders. The entire surface seethes with water. Marching through rocky areas requires continuous negotiation with the route ahead. But stoop down and the detail becomes more astonishing still. Here in this huge landscape, the tiniest flowers thrive. Hywel pointed out the aconites and the sorrel. The little white petals were everywhere in the wet tussocks of grass between the shattered rock. I thought we might find the lily there. But Hywel said no, and we scrambled higher.

High on the wall above us was a large white shape. "Ice," said Hywel. "The sun hardly shines down into this valley and so the snow lingers here." And there was also a certain acidity to the limestone to be noted. "It is these combinations that create the special conditions for the lily," he continued.

Hywel was now directing me like a child looking for an Easter egg. "Up, go on, up a bit."

And then, magically, there it was. In a cleft in a rock, swaying slightly in the wind: a delicate flower on a couple of inches of stalk. The light was still low and the sun shone through the petals. It was the perfect time to find the Snowdon Lily. For most of the year it simply looks like a long strand of grass, easily missed, until it blooms in May and June.

"How many petals can you see?" Asked Hywel.

"Six,"

"And what do the leaves look like?"

They were spikey and quite dark. "They look like chives," I said.

"Well that directly corresponds with the Welsh name, "the rush leaves of the mountain".

Botanists have established the flower as an ice age relict. It wasn't that tourists had picked them all. In our post-ice age period they had always been rare. The first record of the Snowdon Lily in Great Britain was made by the Welsh botanist Edward Llwyd in 1682. There are varieties in Asia and the Alps but this one, in this valley, on the slopes of this mountain, is genetically unique and it is understood that there are fewer than 100 remaining. Some predict that, with global warming, the plant is threatened and will become extinct.

For the time being, however, the lily enjoys the cold, icy conditions of Cwm Idwal. The bright day and the sea shining like the Aegean almost mocked its existence. It was exquisite and defiantly alive, bobbing in solitary fragile prettiness on its broken rocky pinnacle. I felt privileged to see it: a survivor in a popular place, cold and inaccessible. A conundrum in itself.

# –7–
# ANGLESEY
## WILDLIFE

# – ROUND THE ISLAND –

Anglesey is easy to identify, if difficult to pin down. The island juts off the top of mainland Wales in a wide, broken blob of land. Turn around in the middle of its flat plain on a sunny day (and I was blessed with the weather of heaven on my visit) and you encounter the eternal blue rump of Snowdonia, the beginning of mainland Wales proper, rising up on the horizon behind you.

Is Anglesey particularly Welsh? The ports are connected with the Mersey. Its name is Viking in origin. It is mentioned in history because of the attentions of Italians (or Romans as they were known then). And to cap that, it is full of English people.

When had I been before? Back in 2004, I came to the sand dunes at the south end of the island to visit Newborough. This was home to the "Prichard Jones Institute", built by a Welsh retailer who was the Jones half of "Dickins and Jones". The store had an all-you-can eat buffet that impressed me at the age of eleven (when I wanted to eat all I could if I could). With the money made from bug-eyed consumers like me, Jones had in the early years of the twentieth century built a library and reading room for his home town that later needed saving by *Restoration*. It was a quiet town and an interesting place, but few wanted to vote for it.

Somewhere further down that southern coast I had also been to stay with an old friend called Peter. Peter is an agent these days. His white cottage was filled with seaside boat-bits and fishing lines, deckchairs and slip-on sandals. I realised that I had never really thought of him as Welsh. We shared a university, a career and friends, but when we went together to Bangor that afternoon, both to be awarded honorary degrees, he got up and thanked everybody in the Welsh language. Embarrassingly, I couldn't match him. But Peter understood. He had lived here. He may have sounded like a bogus Taff, as I do, but he knew how deeply Welsh Anglesey and the whole region really was.

At some point in my jumbled past, I also climbed the Parys Mountain. I did this to marvel at the pitted, moonface landscape of the place, and four thousand years of copper mining. The copper mine on Anglesey was once one of the largest in the world. The industry was only brought to an end in our own era. Tacitus recounts that copper was actually the reason the Romans came here to fight the Druids and their bare-breasted woman attendants.

I was back in Anglesey and Amlwch a few years later. Again, I got a different take on the same place. The deep harbour at Amlwch, once busy with ore transporters, once boasting its own copper currency, was a steep sided tidal hole where I boarded a pilot ship, climbing down a 30-foot ladder in the darkness before dawn, to go out and meet a container vessel on her way into Liverpool.

What I remember about that adventure, however, was the dash across the countryside in the dead of night, through deep lanes and a maze-like network of narrow roadways, under thick hedges and past sleeping farms, to get to the little port. It seemed to take us forever.

A tangled, remote place? This was something new to me, and perhaps for many others, because, for the casual visitor, Anglesey is defined by the A55, which forms part of the European route E22, at more than 5000km one of the longest of European roads, starting in Russia and crossing Latvia, Sweden, Germany and the Netherlands. No wonder the island can feel like an adjunct to a ferry service: a mere last, flat, small thing to be hurried through before you hit the Irish ferry at Holyhead. Ever since Thomas Telford built his suspension bridge, which was, anyway, just part of a great scheme to reduce travel time from 36 hours to 27 and allow Irish MPs easy access to their representations in London, the island seems to have been treated as a staging post, but Anglesey is huge and wild and rural too.

## – FISH TRAP –

I started in a trap. It looked like a house on a rock, but it was built to be a giant fishing net to gather the herring passing through the Menai Straits, which separate Anglesey from the rest of Wales.

Ynys Gored Goch, on its island in the middle of the rushing tide to the south of the Menai bridge, doesn't get as many herring these days. They have always been fickle, herring. They left the Welsh coast long ago. In the Middle Ages they would have blamed witchcraft. Today we rely on climate change. But I had been told that the fish trap still functioned. It was going to provide breakfast at the start of my journey.

"This place used to be owned by the Bishop of Bangor," another Peter, the owner, told me as we walked out along a curving sea wall that

# ANGLESEY

POPULATION: 69,751

SIZE: 714 SQ KM.

IT'S ESTIMATED THAT THERE ARE 270,000 SHEEP ON THE ISLAND.

ROUGHLY A THIRD OF THE ISLAND IS DESIGNATED AN AREA OF OUTSTANDING NATURAL BEAUTY.

BIRDS YOU CAN SEE: CHOUGH, GUILLEMOT, PEREGRINE, PUFFIN, RAZORBILL.

HOLYHEAD MOUNTAIN IS THE HIGHEST POINT ON THE ISLAND AT 720FT.

THE LARGEST TOWN ON ANGLESEY IS HOLYHEAD (POP: 11,431).

HOLYHEAD COUNTY SCHOOL WAS BRITAIN'S FIRST PROPER COMPREHENSIVE SCHOOL WHEN HOLYHEAD GRAMMAR AND ST CYBI CENTRAL SCHOOL WERE AMALGAMATED IN 1949.

THERE ARE THREE MAJOR WIND FARMS ON ANGLESEY.

BEFORE TELFORD'S A55 ROAD WAS BUILT IT WAS SUCH A DANGEROUS JOURNEY THAT THERE WAS A MAXIMUM SPEED OF SEVEN AND HALF MILES AN HOUR FOR COACHES.

TELFORD'S ROAD STARTS AT MARBLE ARCH IN LONDON, AND ENDS WITH A LESS GRAND COPY OF 'ADMIRALTY ARCH' IN HOLYHEAD HARBOUR.

THOMAS TELFORD'S DESIGNS WERE SO AHEAD OF HIS TIME THAT ABOUT 40% OF THE ROAD HE BUILT STILL SURVIVES IN MUCH THE SAME WAY AS ORIGINALLY DESIGNED.

projected into the strait. "It was largely built 400 years ago. His Grace came here to write his sermons."

Bangor is about three miles to the north on the mainland side. I couldn't imagine the Bishop himself scooping up his breakfast, but he might have had encouraging thoughts on the last supper, or the feeding of the five thousand, or even the fishing of souls.

I deeply wanted to see the trap in action, but I had come at the wrong stage of the tide and too early in the season. Peter was patient. He explained that we could have opened the oak lock-gates that allowed the water to enter and shut the ones at the other end, thus marooning any fish that entered the trap. But it would have been useless. We might even have opened the wall-gates and released the water, in the hope of stranding our prey on the bare rocks. But we would have been disappointed. There simply were no fish.

In the early twentieth century, it was fashionable for visitors to cross to the island to enjoy whitebait teas. They would walk down to the shore by a footpath through the Coed Môr woods, ring a bell placed on the shore for the purpose, and a boat would pull out from the island to collect them. But recently the weather had been cold and wet. Thanks to the delayed winter, the fish just weren't ready to take part in our late medieval industrial hoovering system, even for televisual purposes. Peter regularly caught more than he could gather, but not today.

I did at least discover my challenge disguised as a message in a bottle bobbing about in the lagoon. And I took a little stroll around this isolated kingdom, poised as it was, halfway between the wooded banks of the mainland and Anglesey Island. The Menai is wholly tidal, with strange currents, and the sea surges in from both ends and makes swirling eddies and dangerous whirlpools on the black, glistening surface. The difficulty of the waters caused the HMS Conway to sink there in 1953 and at times of low tide, it's said, you can still see the remains.

Our tour took us round the neat paths and tiny lawns across the little island, and down to what I assumed, from the number of gates, sluices and locks, was an entirely different fish trap to the east. This one was a project in hand. Peter had bought this island in order to conserve and restore it. He escaped here at weekends from a property restoration business he ran in the Wirral. Inside, his main cottage had the proportions of a large boat. Outside there were borders of flowers and neat trees, which overhung whitewashed walls. In the early morning's blazing sunshine I could have been in Greece.

Despite the continuous presence of human beings since deepest history (we were close to the point where the Roman legionaries had forded the stream to grapple with the last of the rebellious Welsh) sea birds still behaved as if we had never arrived.

"Over there in the border," Peter whispered "you can see the oystercatcher nest."

I looked, and in a rough bundle of grass and straw amongst the perennials under the kitchen window sat a couple of coffee-coloured eggs.

"The mother and father are just over there waiting for us to go." Peter pointed across at the rocks, where two oystercatchers were bobbing about, 20 feet from where we were standing. "If we go inside, they'll go back and she can resume sitting, but she won't do that if we stay here."

So we went inside and had a cup of tea. Then we had toast. And some croissants. The oystercatchers returned to their nest and I met Peter's wife and his friends. And I forgot about the whitebait.


## – PUFFINS –

My message in a bottle was to try to "spot a puffin". I am not a twitcher, but I was prepared to make an exception for this bird. It rather excited me. To begin with, the puffin has an exotic, highly-coloured beak. Often the rarest and most inaccessible birds turn out to be drab, unexciting creatures. A puffin is almost a parrot by comparison. In fact one of its nicknames is the 'parrot of the sea' or the 'clown of the sea'.

Further study revealed that it has a mysterious side too. It lives in burrows; often burrows vacated by rabbits. But it only stays on the land for a short time, around four months, and then only in order to breed. The rest of the year the noble, if tiny, puffin heads off to sea and despite its puny dimensions and slightly fragile, nay delicate, nay ornamental, appearance lives on the wing out in the stormy North Atlantic. No wonder island dwellers thought it was really a form of flying fish and regularly ate it, especially at Lent and on Fridays to avoid meat-prohibition by the Catholic Church.

Having missed out on whitebait, I suppose I could have eaten a puffin myself. But Welsh puffins are quite properly protected from the most vigorous appetite. Puffins themselves eat fish (I wonder if they are to blame for the lack of herring). They usually catch around 10 fish per trip,

# SUSPENSION BRIDGES

BEFORE THE BRITANNIA AND MENAI BRIDGES WERE BUILT THE ONLY WAY ACROSS THE TREACHEROUS MENAI STRAITS WAS VIA FERRY OR AT TIMES OF LOW TIDE BY FOOT.

---

IN 1775 A BOAT CARRYING 55 PEOPLE BECAME STRANDED ON A SAND BAR IN THE MIDDLE OF THE STRAIT. HIGH WINDS AND TREACHEROUS CONDITIONS MEANT THAT A RESCUE ATTEMPT HAD TO BE ABANDONED. ONLY ONE PERSON SURVIVED THE DISASTER.

---

THE DRUIDS WERE ABLE TO MAKE ANGLESEY THEIR MOST REMOTE REFUGE WITH THE MENAI STRAITS ACTING LIKE A CASTLE MOAT PROTECTING THE ISLAND FROM INVADERS.

---

BOTH BRIDGES HAD TO HAVE THE DECK AT LEAST 100FT ABOVE HIGH WATER TO ENSURE SHIPS COULD PASS UNDERNEATH IT.

---

THERE WERE FOUR LIMESTONE LION STATUES ON THE ENTRANCES TO BRITANNIA BRIDGE. THEY WERE CARVED BY JOHN THOMAS, WHO ALSO DID STONE CARVINGS FOR BUCKINGHAM PALACE AND THE HOUSES OF PARLIAMENT. THE LIONS ARE NOW SITUATED FORLORNLY BELOW THE ROAD SURFACE.

---

THE TUBULAR DESIGN OF STEPHENSON'S BRIDGE WENT ON TO INFLUENCE MANY OTHER BRIDGE DESIGNERS, INCLUDING BRUNEL, AND ITS PRINCIPLES ARE STILL WIDELY USED TODAY.

though the record in Britain is a whopping 60 fish at once.

Peter helped me to board a local tourist rib from one of his three or four available slipways or jetties and we shot away. The mountains of Eryri gleamed in the sun. The boat charged up the strait, blasting under the Telford Suspension Bridge, one of the great engineering feats of its time, condemned as ugly by some, but rightly hailed by Southey, the great Romantic poet, as the symbol of the spirit of the age.

It took 150 men using a pulley system to raise the 23.5-ton chains to the top of the tower in 1826. They had to repeat this 15 times to get the remaining chains in place. Not surprisingly, a large crowd gathered to watch the first being got up and they cheered wildly as the connection was made.

The bridge is also mentioned in a Lewis Carroll poem in *Through The Looking Glass* – the White Knight says to Alice:

> *I heard him then, for I had just completed my design*
> *To keep the Menai Bridge from rust*
> *By boiling it in wine.*

It wasn't boiled in wine, however, but linseed oil.

The western bank flashed past. It was lined with large suburban villas lurking in the trees. More rich incomers, I supposed. Bangor swooped by on the south. We bounced on, quickly overhauling a solid-looking, industrial fishing boat.

"Mussels," Charlie, my skipper, shouted at me. The Menai Strait's unique topography is perfect for mussel-farming and Anglesey is home to the country's biggest mussel farm, providing around three quarters of our farmed mussels. The estuary opened out to either side, the Anglesey shore now sporting low, greenish hills; the landward side stepping back from the coast to higher, blue parapets. To our right, the mound of what appeared to be a tall, domineering island swung into view. It was in fact the peninsula headland of the Great Orme, joined to the mainland by an invisible low spit. I was due to explore that on another occasion.

Now we hugged the Anglesey coast. Beyond Beaumaris, we shot past a few weathered old industrial buildings and powered on towards the 69 acres of Puffin Island, ninth largest off the coast of Wales, and a long high-backed lozenge, pointing north. This seemed like the obvious place to fulfill my quest.

On the eastern side we slowed and crept in towards a layered ragged cliff of carboniferous limestone, with the engines gurgling like washing machines. Above us a great rookery of birds swept restlessly back and forth. Charlie shouted out their identities. "Guillemots! Cormorants! Razorbill! Kittiwake!!"

"Puffins?"

"No."

Things might have been easier 200 years ago when (it has been estimated) 50,000 puffins lived on this island. Gradually the numbers reduced. It was not simply that locals found them a delicacy. The truth was that the island was swarming with rats. By the twenty-first century around only twenty breeding pairs remained. Perhaps to avoid having to rename the place "Rat Island", the Countryside Council of Wales intervened and set about poisoning the rodents. Whether this encouraged the twenty pairs to continue breeding I do not know.

"Razorbill! Guillemot! Flamingo!" I was randomly shouting out the names of the other birds, but still I couldn't spot a "Fratercula". The puffin's Latin name means "little brother", because it clasps its feet together as if in prayer when it takes to the air. The island had been a haven for real monks, big brothers, since the sixth century, but both now seemed to have left.

It wasn't a wasted trip. It was a fabulous trip. At the north end we passed close to an exposed ledge, where fat, furry seals lay uncomfortably on the rocks and strained upwards, in inverted ungainly bows, turning their dog-like faces to check us out, like nudists surprised by interlopers

Tommy, who had joined us for the journey, voiced his approbation. "I have never seen this," he said. "I've worked on Anglesey for five years now, but I never knew any of this was here."

We rounded the northern tip and chugged back, through deeper water, even spotting rare human beings on the eastern cliff top. "You can go as part of a guided tour,' said Charles, but you're not supposed to land without permission."

He pushed his throttle forward and we roared back to Beaumaris where he put me ashore alongside a flotilla of visiting yachts that seemed to have come from Northern Ireland. "What are you up to, eh?" they shouted.

"Nothing," I shouted back through fixed teeth, trying to remain disengaged for the camera.

There is something satisfying about landing in a seaside town from a boat, as long as you manage to do so safely. On the way back, Charles pointed out the sites of various wrecks that had failed to make the entrance to the strait and come a cropper on the great shallow expanses of sand that ran away towards Bangor. Somewhere out there were the three wrecks that all went down on the same day, December 5th, though separated by many hundreds of years. All these ships lost all hands, save for one person. And that one survivor, spookily, was called Hugh Williams, in each case.

The only Hugh Williams I know changed his name to Hugh Bonneville, and went on to skipper Downton Abbey. I hope Hugh has the good sense to remember who he really is if he ever finds himself in a winter storm in the Menai Straits.

The pier where we landed once greeted paddle steamers from the Liverpool and North Wales Steamship Company, bringing tourists from the Mersey. I strolled down the springy planks, past the day-trippers and the ice cream guzzlers, and into Beaumaris itself.

This was my first real encounter with Anglesey on this trip. The town appeared to be a neat Georgian-looking box, but it was built in 1295 to accompany the castle, regarded by many as the pinnacle of James of St George's career and the low point of Welsh independence. It was part of the ring of iron, the circle of fortresses designed to put us Welsh in our place. Beaumaris Castle is described by many as the most technically perfect castle in Britain.

Strolling amongst the Lancashire accents, I wondered how many realised that Welsh people themselves were once banned from the town: a sort of outpost in the injun territory, like a cowboy fort. For centuries the Welsh were not allowed to buy property in the borough. Perhaps that's why they still seemed to keep a low profile.

A paper poster outside a newsagent's informed me of the "N.WAKE QUAKE": a reference I think to the earthquake that had recently rocked Llŷn in N. Wales. Inside I picked up a glossy magazine that boasted (on its cover) that one of the best places to find puffins in Britain was on South Stack in Anglesey, and I chatted with the proprietress. Olwen happily corrected me on my would-be French pronunciation. The Welsh call it "Bew-mariss" she told me. This was despite the fact that it got its name from the Norman occupiers who in 1300 had thought the site was a rather attractive bog, or "beau marais".

Olwen explained that Welsh was her first language. That, despite appearances, and despite the tourists, the incomers and the holiday cottages and English entrepreneurs running power-ribs, restaurants and antique shops, the heart of Anglesey was deeply Welsh. She herself lived outside the town. I don't think this was because of any old medieval rules,

# PUFFIN ISLAND
# AND PUFFINS

THE WELSH NAME FOR PUFFIN ISLAND,
YNYS SEIRIOL, REFERS TO SAINT
SEIRIOL, WHO ESTABLISHED A
MONASTIC SETTLEMENT ON THE ISLAND.

---

THERE ARE FOUR DIFFERENT TYPES OF PUFFIN:
THE ATLANTIC PUFFIN, THE HORNED PUFFIN,
THE TUFTED PUFFIN AND RHINOCEROS PUFFIN.

---

THE PUFFIN CAN FLY AT UP TO 55MPH.
AT THIS SPEED WINGS CAN REACH UP TO
400 BEATS PER MINUTES (SO FAST THEY
BECOME A BLUR).

---

PUFFINS ARE SPECIALLY ADAPTED TO
LIFE AT SEA, THEY HAVE WATERPROOF FEATHERS
AND CAN DRINK SALT WATER. THEY CAN DIVE
UP TO 60M UNDERWATER.

---

WHEN A PUFFIN IS BORN IT STAYS IN ITS
BURROW FOR AROUND 45 DAYS TILL IT
CAN FLY, THEN IT HEADS OUT TO SEA FOR THE
NEXT THREE TO FIVE YEARS WHERE IT LEARNS HOW
TO FISH AND CHOOSES A MATE FOR LIFE.

but old habits linger on in rural Wales. The conquest of the late thirteenth century is talked about as if it happened a few months ago. The English are still held to account. Mind you, I would have thought that the French origins of the town's name might have fingered the real villains: those blasted, avaricious, bastard Normans.

Olwen was happy to tell me that the only Welsh word I regularly heard in my house: "bach" as in "Griffith bach!" expressed usually in tones of huge sorrow, meant "little", (I always assume it meant "darling".) So I was little Griffith whenever I cut the heads off the tulips or broke those windows round the back of my friend's farm or hit my sister. But I also discovered that if I wanted to find South Stack I would have to follow the coast along the southerly side.

## – SALT-WATER TAFFY –

I retraced my route, but this time on land, skirting the south shore of the island and taking a bus through the leafy parkland round the back of Plas Newydd – "At the house there is also a Military Museum which contains campaign relics belonging to the first Marquess of Anglesey, mementos of the Battle of Waterloo and the Anglesey leg," I read.

Lord Uxbridge's famous articulated false leg on show in Anglesey's stately home was built to replace the original, which became a tourist attraction in Belgium after it was amputated and buried under a willow tree. I would rather have liked to see the hallowed fake limb but we had no time. ITV wouldn't pay for visits to great houses and, besides, I was meeting a man about some salt.

I found him waist-deep on an unprepossessing beach. He was peering into an instrument that measured the salinity of the water in his inlet pipe. "Halen Môn" produces an upmarket condiment extracted from the strait. I was a little surprised by this news.

"Surely, I said, swinging a hand over the horizon, "that's Caernarfon over there". They have pipes leading down to the water too, don't they? Aren't they, ahem, putting stuff in as opposed to taking it out."

David was not fazed. "The water here is exceptionally pure, salty Welsh seawater," he assured me, "and the action of the strait and the tide rushing through it effectively…" he chose his words carefully "…flushes it out, on a daily basis."

We strolled back towards his factory premises. Not bad, considering he originally started with a saucepan on the Aga. Fifteen years before, he had boiled down a pint or so of local seawater to produce some particularly fine-looking crystals; he sold them to a local butcher and now exports to twenty-two countries. David was another incomer. He originally studied at Bangor University across on the mainland, and I congratulated him on staying over to exploit the wild freedoms of Wales.

"Not so free." He explained. "In fact my pipe crosses the tidal regions to get into deep water and that is the property of the crown. They charge me for extracting the water."

The Crown Commissioners have become rather commercially minded of late. The water in the sea is not owned by Her Majesty, but a pipe to get at it has to cross the intertidal foreshore and that is.

Nonetheless, seawater was a minor part of David's costs. Inside the sheds was a sequence of evaporating pans. I had to encase myself in a beard snood, a blue net that promised to contain my facial hair as I watched the snowy crystals being shovelled into buckets.

Whether as a result of secret processes or extra salinity, the long white fragile flakes had a crunchy purity that far outshone salt from the mines of Chester, or Siberia, or wherever else we get it these days. I stood quietly to one side in a palely lit enclosure while a member of staff, almost unidentifiable in his snoods, gently lifted crumbling and fragile cascades of the crystals out of the evaporating pans with a shovel.

Môn is part of the Welsh name for Anglesey: "Ynys Môn", and the syllable derives from the Roman name for the island: Mona. Here they are again, those Romans. They seem to be part of every story round here. Of course, the Romans made salt in their pans by similar methods. Perhaps they had a yen for crunchy condiments too, but I have read that salt is salt. Despite the foodie's delight in Japanese smoked salt or Arctic salt or even Welsh sea salt, it is, essentially, sodium chloride. Or is it?

While we waited to move on towards South Stack, we spent a few minutes in the "showroom", admiring the pure white pottery jars and the bright blue labels, brilliantly designed to capture the tang of the sea. But it's the crisp and gleaming crystals of the product itself that are really attractive. This is salt with crunch, salt with texture, sodium chloride with some of the magic of natural geometry built into its creation. Halen Môn was taking something industrial and repackaging it for a new upmarket, discerning, sophisticated world here on Anglesey. They even provide a recipe for a pigeon dish, accompanied with chocolate, vanilla Halen Môn and fig marmalade – no help cooking puffins though.

## – JESUS WANTS ME –

David had offered to take me on to my next appointment and get me that bit closer to South Stack. He started up his 1920s Austin Sunbeam. Jimmy the Jack Russell jumped up on the dickie seat and barked whimpering approval as we rumbled off, through the close-hedged country lanes, across the great flat interior plateau of the island. David extolled his lifestyle. He felt himself lucky to be able to live in such rural bliss, and run a business, cut off from some of the pressures of the mainland.

We pootled on at 20 miles an hour and stopped by a farm gate to make contact with our cameraman. As we stood in the road, some five of us, talking with the owner of the farm, a big black BMW shot round a corner at speed. Far from slowing down, it accelerated towards us, threading its way though us with inches to spare at nearly 50 miles an hour.

"Probably lost tourists," someone said.

## – WILD LAND ROVERS –

The tourists may have been looking for the nearby Tacla Taid Museum. That is where we were heading now, the Jack Russell sliding about on uncut claws as we turned into a farm and, next to it, a bare concrete courtyard littered with huge vehicles where David abandoned me. I was pointed towards a big green corrugated iron shed in search of Arfon, the owner.

Arfon was a never-throw-anything-away man, of the best sort. Charming, diffident and the second solidly Welsh person I had met so far on Anglesey, his motor museum, now a successful tourist attraction, had been the only available solution after his private collection of rescued vehicles began to outgrow his garden. Tacla Taid is the largest museum of its kind in Wales.

He started with a tractor. Having learned to drive at the age of eight, at fifteen he was given an old Massey Ferguson, which he rebuilt and then used as his personal transport. Now he greeted me warmly in the middle of a landscape of glinting chrome. We were on the ground floor of the building: a monument to the popular car. There were dozens of Morrises, Citroëns and Rovers. Most of them had been brought in by farmers or local people – nothing too fancy. These weren't Maseratis or Ferraris. There was even the brother to my dad's old Morris Oxford, in exactly the same shade of grey.

"They are essentially simple pieces of technology," Arfon told me. "That's their great virtue. You lift a bonnet now and it is all sealed away, but in the old days you could repair any car if you had a mind to it."

Or any vehicle, I assumed. On the upper level of the shed stood an array of tractors. "Ah yes," I said boldly, "Tractor heaven. I have one of these at home." I proudly slapped my hand on to the flimsy metal engine-cover of a Massey Ferguson.

"That's a 1956 petrol-driven Massey." Arfon said.

"Oh." I was abashed. "Mine's a diesel-driven 1963."

'You mean one like this," said Arfon. He took me over to another vehicle, three tractors down the row.

But I wasn't there to admire the tractors, or the huge military cranes, or the two Vauxhall Carltons – ugly beasts from the nineties, which were developed to be the fastest full four-seater cars on the road and still brought a tear to Arfon's eye (nothing Italianate about them, I guessed). I was there to find a humble "Land Rover Series One." Sure enough, Arfon had a fine specimen. A stout green box on wheels, standing by the shed door.

This vehicle, which revolutionised life for the British farmer, was born here in Anglesey. It started as a notion of Rover's chief engineer Maurice Wilks. He originally drew a sketch of his concept in 1947 in the sand of Red Wharf Bay, a few miles from where we stood. He took a Rover engine and stuck it into the jeep and tested the thing in Tros Yr Afon. The hybrid, all-terrain workhorse rumbled on its way. Over four million have subsequently been made. 65 percent are still working.

I was expecting the first model to be a brutish thing, ready to clamber up the 700-foot mountains of Anglesey, but it felt oddly slight.

While Arfon's helper raised the shutters for us, I guided the Land Rover out and onto the road, heading west for South Stack. The gear stick needed an element of gentlemanly negotiation, like a drunk being persuaded to go in through the door. You didn't want to push too hard. Just help it in the general direction and, yup, it got there. The cabin seemed to be a little loose on the chassis, but that was a natural wobble.

Arfon sat beside me, beaming with pleasure at the sheer excellence of the thing. He loved its straightforwardness. He revelled in its quiet purposefulness. He chuckled out loud as a man on a bicycle defiantly overtook us and he urged me on, as we came down the hill to a deserted beach, mounted over a mini dune, and slithered across a bank of stones down towards the sea.

"Are we going to do this?" I asked.

"That's what she's made for," he said.

I stopped on the sand.

When we needed to do it all over again for the camera, several times, Arfon was happy to leap out and adjust the differential locks on the wheels. He let me dig her out of a spin and run her back and forth on the perilous descent. She still had plenty of muscle in her, but not in a showy way, just quietly capable, even if a push-bike was faster. And, clearly, that was what Arfon admired most of all. She was "proper".

I stood back and watched as Arfon reversed her one more time and drove away up the hill: Welsh grunt.

## – LIME WASH –

A small squared-off building sat on a mound of land in the middle of the waste of a wide bay. It was glowing in the sunshine. It was called St Cwyfan's. Originally founded in the seventh century, the church I was walking towards had been built in the thirteenth century.  It was about a quarter of a mile away. The foreshore I was crossing had once all been land. I was able to appreciate the power and wildness of Anglesey's south coast, which faces down St George's Channel towards the mouth of the Atlantic at the southern end of Ireland, because fields, which once joined this nodule of earth to the rest of Anglesey, had been utterly swept away by successive storms 400 years ago. The island continued to erode until the end of the nineteenth century when an architect called Harold Hughes from Llanfairfechan raised the money to protect it. He made a retaining wall around the remaining cake of island and restored the church.

Now, as I walked up the steps I passed a sign warning me of the danger of being stranded (and, indeed, of stepping backwards to get a good view of the simple building). I was greeted by the volunteers who had gathered to limewash the walls.

# THE LAND ROVER

MAURICE WILKS CONCEIVED THE IDEA
FOR THE LAND ROVER ON HIS FARM IN ANGLESEY
IN 1947, HE WAS ALSO RESPONSIBLE FOR
THE FIRST GAS TURBINE DRIVEN CAR.

---

48 PROTOTYPES WERE BUILT BEFORE PRODUCTION
OFFICIALLY BEGAN IN 1948.

---

THE FAMILIAR LIGHT GREEN COLOUR
ASSOCIATED WITH THE EARLY LAND ROVER
OWES ITS ORIGIN TO THE WAR – THERE
WAS AN ABUNDANCE OF GREEN AIRCRAFT
PAINT AFTER THE WAR WAS OVER.

---

IT'S CLAIMED THAT ABOUT TWO THIRDS
OF THE ORIGINAL LAND ROVER CARS
ARE STILL WORKING TODAY.

---

THE LAND ROVER RANGE ROVER BRAND
ALSO MAKES BICYCLES AND COFFEE.

---

TATA MOTORS BOUGHT THE PREVIOUSLY
FORD OWNED 'JAGUAR LAND ROVER'
GROUP IN 2009 FOR $2.3 BILLION. FORD
PREVIOUSLY BOUGHT THE GROUP FOR
$2.96 BILLION FROM BMW.

Lime is a magical substance to traditional restorers. "A useful, beautiful and benign natural finish", according to the Society for the Protection of Ancient Buildings, it is catnip to a caring builder. You mix the white powder with water. It starts popping and boiling or "going off", and then it has to be applied to a walled surface. Today it enjoys a fairly sacred status; it wasn't always so. Wordsworth hated the whitewashed cottages in the Lake District.

Personally, I prefer the slightly oatmeal off-white colour that I first encountered on a similar newly-painted chapel in Orkney. I only learned recently that that particular antique look derived from impurities. Today we have to add pigment to get it to that shade. And then we have to slap it on.

The volunteers got me a full coverall, some goggles and a pair of gloves. Lime burns, especially the eyes. Like refugees from CSI on a particularly noxious murder enquiry we paraded out to the side of the church and started applying our milky protection. Limewash hardly adheres to a brush at all. I stuck my frazzled spokes of hair, worn down by previous use, straight into the bucket and lifted out a loose liquid that seemed to pour back as quickly as I transferred it to the wall.

There were two other coats on already. Applying white on white is frustrating. Maybe that's what got Adolf Hitler into a bad mood. The house painter can enjoy the first coat, even relish the second, but lime needs five coats, starting where? Finishing where? Have I done this bit or not? Gradually we worked along the wall, feeling our way more by a sense of dampness then anything else.

Limewash flies in the face of modern convenience. It needs to be replaced every five years, perhaps more quickly if the winds blow in from St George's Channel. If storms can carry away acres of Anglesey they can certainly make short work of a few layers of damp paste. Experts will tell you that lime is best, because it breathes. Sealed-in water does the damage to old buildings. With lime coverings the damp is absorbed – but then evaporates again.

My non-expert eye, however, peering at the wall through dirt-encrusted goggles, valued something else entirely: a living response to the climate. North Wales is sometimes about embracing weather rather than fighting it. The rain and the wind come hurtling in and the side of the chapel of St Cwyfan constantly adapts. It creates a subtle impasto, like the sky in a painting by Boudin. The blank wall becomes a soothing, continually-changing canvas of fading tones.

Can a building aspire to be a living part of the landscape? Yes, if it is constructed out of the rough stones of the cliff and painted with the earth. The old church squatting down in the face of the prevailing weather, hunkered against the storms, felt entirely appropriate to its setting: simple and spiritual, despite its new and gleaming paint job.

Now I was due to continue with the help of a cycling club from Aberffraw. They started me off in gentle cycling country in the dunes of the south coast, and then let me wander across the island on my own.

## – THROUGH THE MILL –

Halfway to my next destination, I paused in a green lane by a hedge in a road shadowed by trees. A gravelled drive ran off to the south, leading to a hidden large farmhouse. The wind rustled through the leafy tunnel above me and I hiked the bike over to a gate to gaze across a pasture to cattle and a serene, rural idyll. We were a long way from the tourist edges of Anglesey now and in the heart of Ynys Môn. This Welsh Anglesey is also known as Mam Cymru, "the mother of Wales".

Living in a post-industrial technical world (in which we are happy to eat avocados from Israel and arrange cut flowers from Kenya) it is sometimes difficult to appreciate how important simple agricultural fertility once was. Humans radically changed their expectations and found ways of controlling their environment less than three hundred years ago. Before that, for the previous six thousand years, Anglesey represented true wealth. There was no sense of it being "a quiet and remote spot". It was Mam Cymru. It was "the mother" of the nation because of its reputed capacity to feed the whole of Wales. These rich flat fields were like Sicily to Rome – the granary – the supply store of the country. There were once 50 windmills scattered across the elevated plain of the island to serve that harvest. Now only one remains: Melin Llynnon.

I cycled on, turned a corner and quickly spotted it ahead, standing out on a prominent hillock, 30 feet high and whitewashed, with a straight row of square windows leading up to a conical, tiled roof.

I was well ahead of the camera crew now. They wanted to get some shots of me from a distance. The site itself was breezy. There were high washed clouds. I poked my head into the first building I came to, and two women in pinafores looked up from their baking.

"Oh, we are expecting you," said the older one. "Look. We're just making your lunch."

Built in 1775, the mill still grinds corn, and the flour is used in the bread and cakes served in the café. Its great sails continued to turn until 1924. A storm damaged the cap in 1918 so that it couldn't turn to the wind, but it was used for a further six years whenever there was a south-west wind. It was bought in 1978 and restored by an enlightened council.

Lloyd, who met me up by the great white pepper pot itself, was preparing to close up. He was going to give me a lift to South Stack, but before he did that, he wanted to secure his machinery. Like a tall sailing ship, the power he routinely employed was immense and unpredictable. The design of the mill, which may seem Heath Robinson to us, was ingenious and precise. It used an exact technical knowledge of the capacities and limits of timber, the strength of the wind, and the capacity of the engine. It is no surprise that millers were at the forefront of industrialisation. But for this operation, he had me to help him.

Lloyd needed to lock down his sails at the right angle to the wind. There was a short piece of wood sticking out of the lower sail near to the centre of the apex. Having determined the wind direction and allowed the sails to back round so that they faced the "wrong" way, he asked me to flick a rope over this wooden protrusion, in order for him to tie the system off. It was 15 feet above my head. I needed to get a wave to travel along the rope and then loop that wave over the stick with a flick of my wrist. Lloyd showed me how to do it, pretty much with his hand behind his back, while talking to me. Then he left me to it.

Sometimes a principle can be totally comprehensible and yet impossible to perform. Years of throwing rope on boats meant that I understood how rope behaves, but the actuality of flicking the bottom of the rope and twisting it to one side, exactly in sequence, so that the slack travelling hump of rope danced to one side as it reached the top became frustrating. Eight times I nearly did it. Nearly is not enough. Lloyd meanwhile ran around his windmill attending to other business and as he passed me on one of his circumnavigations took it out of my hands and did it in one. Then he disentangled it and handed the rope back to me.

I think I did it on twist and flick number 16. And from then on I could do it every time.

Having disengaged the sails we now had to block the machinery. We went into the shell of the building, climbing upwards on narrow stairs past the carefully organised elements of the mill system. The power from the turning sails is translated to the mill wheels. But it is also used to perform all the other heavy functions of the mill. It runs a winch that lifts the sacks of corn to the very top of the building. The force of gravity can be used to separate and control the feed to the wheels. Right up in the attic under the hat of the roof we finally came to a significant and impressive piece of wooden Meccano. Vast cogs translated the horizontal turn of the sail shaft into the vertical turn of a post through the middle of the building.

Lloyd now scampered around this fearsome engine. He jumped over blocks and stepped across an open void. He encouraged me to follow him and we took up station in front of the massive piece of clockwork. The idea was to apply a chock or brake, and the active part of the brake was a long, heavy balk of timber. By jamming this into the mechanism it would prevent it turning. But I was lifting the long heavy piece of timber by one end only. The other end waved hopelessly about.

"Go on, you've got it," said Lloyd.

I didn't think I had, but I pushed it forward and it seemed to lodge in the gap.

"That's great," said Lloyd and led me outside onto a small balcony.

We gazed out over the sweep of Anglesey. Lloyd pointed to the hilly west where I was heading, up a steady slope, to get to the high cliffs of South Stack. We turned to look north, where the very technology that we had just settled for the night was entering a new phase. The bay was littered with wind turbines. Not many were turning.

You might have expected Lloyd, a miller, and a man who learned his trade anew in order to run the only working mill in Wales, to be an advocate of wind power and he was, for his purposes. He ground corn when the wind blew. Windmills once dominated the fens in the East of England. Similarly, they pumped when the wind blew. Both these local sources of power were used intermittently. They provided their locally required power in bursts of energy as it was needed.

Lloyd shook his head. Wind suits the needs of any system that can wait and work as required. Over a period of time the wind will blow enough to pump the fens dry and enough to deal with a harvest. But we cannot currently store electricity in any meaningful way. He wondered whether those wind machines we were looking at could ever be more than a partial solution to our current power needs.

Meanwhile we had to get on. South Stack was some miles to the west and as Lloyd pointed out, we hadn't had lunch yet.

# – TO THE LIGHTHOUSE –

At some point we transferred from one island to another: Holy Island. I must have missed the bridge on the roadway. We were suddenly simply there, at South Stack.

I stood on a high cliff looking out over the sea. I was high up again. The top of the lighthouse was way below me. The bare outcrops of the cliff tops were covered with wild flowers and seabirds circled beneath my feet.

A beautiful staircase led downwards, wheeling in slithering bends, so I took it for 400 steps through smooth-walled ramparts to a rugged, bolted metal-truss bridge, which crossed a sea gorge and deposited me on my ultimate Welsh island in the west: Ynys Lawd. The cover photo for Roxy Music's *Siren* album was taken directly below the bridge to South Stack – Bryan Ferry's idea, apparently.

This place had been home to keepers as recently as 1984. Now the light is fully automated. The keepers had left the terraced row of whitewashed houses next to the light tower earlier, because the location was considered unsafe for children, but the steep walled rock remained a self-sufficient village, as much as a sea-mark. High walls protected fields once used for crops, and even now they were thick with what looked like overgrown cabbages: a surreal organic element, like a 1940s painting.

Amongst these burgeoning vegetables and down in the tufts of coarse grass by the approach paths, hundreds of gulls were nesting, within metres of tourists like me. They lay still and beady-eyed. Their mates jumped on the walls and croaked open-mouthed aggression. Like my fish-trap island, the wild and the occupied coexisted here. Men were mere intruders, and just about tolerated.

Glancing in amongst the glaucous, forgotten house vegetables, I could see the yellow-rimmed eyes and the red-darted heads swivelling to watch me. Close up, the birds were more arrogantly perfect than they appear when they soar in flocks, or bomb rubbish tips. Herring gulls may be scavengers, there may be thousands of them, but they repay close attention. They are wind-tunnel designed: lean, jet-blasted creatures decked out in dazzling white and startling flecks of colour like a painter's contrasting highlights. I was satisfied already. This was the Galapagos of the Welsh coast. Any puffin was going to be a bonus.

More steps up the tower, this time on a regular spiral mount to the very top. You don't get any particular vantage point. The cliff top is higher and the island is closer to the rookeries. But the tower has a magnificence of its own. Built in 1808, following the Act of Union, when a Captain Hugh Evans finally persuaded Trinity House that the increased traffic with Ireland required some sort of protection, the light was secured by preparing detailed maps of all the shipwrecks along the coast. (Archaeological evidence shows that people have been sailing from Holyhead to Ireland for the past 4,000 years.) The tower rises 28 metres and is, again, a dazzling white, like the cottages that surround it, like a gull's back, like a breaker on the shore: shining with a clean and fresh seaside brilliance.

At the very top of the utilitarian hollow stack is a giant Fresnel LED lamp, resting on a bed of mercury, dense enough to support its great weight and yet liquid enough to allow its mass to be revolved. It provides a flash every 10 seconds. In 1831 Captain Evans came up with the unique idea of a moveable light that would shine out closer to the sea surface. A track was built, meaning a cabin on wheels could be lowered to within 12m of sea level to give increased visibility.

On this bright, clear day, with an empty sea ahead, it was difficult to imagine fog. But fog regularly obscured the whole of the headland. Trinity House had felt it necessary to drag another light down to sea level, to put up bells and even to install cannons to warn off shipping. They replaced their oil lights, got bigger gas lights, then bigger electric ones again, with attendant machinery and generators. Today, the ships that pass navigate by satellite and it is only yachtsmen or disabled boats that really need the extra guidance that a lighthouse provides. Instead, the tower has become a beacon for tourists. In the place of keepers there are now permanent guides on watch.

Martyn was there for me, quite prepared to explain the workings and the daring exploits of the former inhabitants of the islands, but I needed his guidance on another matter. He took me to the lantern room and pointed back the way I had come. There was a knot of people halfway down the steps. I might have noticed them myself, if I hadn't been taking the stairs three at a time. They were leaning into the balustrade of one of the hairpin bends and peering at something on the opposite cliff. These were the puffin-watchers.

## – PUFFIN AND PANTIN –

Only eight pairs had returned to South Stack that summer, members of the twitcher group told me when I finally got to them. Perhaps more

# SOUTH STACK

A PETITION TO BUILD A LIGHTHOUSE ON SOUTH STACK WAS PRESENTED TO KING CHARLES II IN 1665. THE PETITION WAS REJECTED AND IT WASN'T TILL 1809 THAT SOUTH STACK EVENTUALLY GOT ITS LIGHTHOUSE.

THE LIGHTHOUSE IS 28M HIGH AND ABOUT 60M ABOVE MEAN WATER LEVEL.

IT WAS DESIGNED BY DAVID ALEXANDER AT A COST OF £12,000.

THE SPIRAL STAIRCASE OF THE LIGHTHOUSE IS BUILT FROM LIMESTONE FROM A QUARRY IN PENMON.

THE ORIGINAL LIGHTHOUSE PRODUCED ITS LIGHT BY 21 OIL LAMPS BACKED BY REFLECTORS 54CM IN DIAMETER.

THERE ARE 400 STEPS TO TAKE YOU DOWN TO THE LIGHTHOUSE ITSELF.

ON 12TH SEPTEMBER 1984, THE LIGHTHOUSE WAS AUTOMATED AND THE KEEPERS WITHDRAWN. THE LIGHT AND FOG SIGNAL ARE NOW REMOTELY CONTROLLED AND MONITORED FROM THE TRINITY HOUSE OPERATIONAL CONTROL CENTRE IN HARWICH, ESSEX.

THE CURRENT LIGHT FLASHES ONCE EVERY TEN SECONDS AND HAS THE INTENSITY OF 467,000 CANDLES, AND CAN BE SEEN FROM 24 MILES AWAY.

THE IRON SUSPENSION BRIDGE LEADING TO THE ISLAND WAS BUILT IN 1828, NEARLY 20 YEARS AFTER THE LIGHTHOUSE WAS BUILT. UNTIL THEN THE ONLY WAY ON TO THE ISLAND FOR PASSENGERS OR SUPPLIES WAS VIA A 21M CABLE WITH A SLIDING BASKET ATTACHED.

would come. Someone loaned me his binoculars. I gazed across at the cliff outcrop beyond, following their minute directions. "Come across from the big rock that looks like a triangle."

They all looked like that.

"But you can see that there is a ledge of grass."

I could.

"You need to get on that, then move to the left and across to the guillemots." As usual there were dozens of other birds fussing about. "Now, go up and you see the four black birds…"

I did.

"Stay on them. There's a burrow just in the shadow there and he seems to have gone in there. If you wait…"

But I didn't have to wait. Almost as I brought my binoculars to bear, a puffin casually hopped out of the dark area and skipped over into the light. I was looking at a bird about the size of a carton of milk. There it was, with a white chest and, clear and perfect, a stripey, multi-coloured beak. It looked so childish and innocent, and we have so readily adopted it as a symbol of the nursery, that it is difficult to accept that this small creature, bobbing about in the pinks, now obviously gathering strands of grass to line its summer nest, was one of the hardiest sea birds, able to live on salt water, consume huge quantities of fish and ride out the boiling ocean storms for months, with far less sustenance and support than the average lighthouse keeper required

But I had definitely seen it. I stayed to watch it launch itself off into the chasm and hurtle down to the blue water 200 feet below. And all on this perfect seaside day. I envied the puffin the swim and their agility and resilience, except that I was enjoying my own human holiday of sun and sea and breeze on Holy Island. The puffins and the gulls, the razorbills and the guillemots would stay there when the night rain slanted in and a front arrived off the Atlantic to drench Anglesey and reassert its wildness.

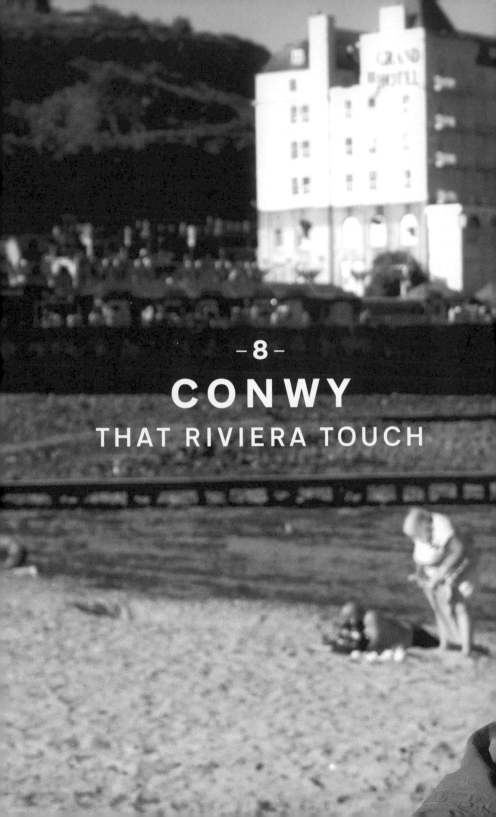

– 8 –

# CONWY

## THAT RIVIERA TOUCH

## – GATEWAY TO THE STARS –

When I finally went into Conwy, across the Telford bridge, the middle way, between the ghastly modern car-crossing and the Stephenson-designed grey-boxed railway bridge, (boxed, alas, so that the passengers don't even glimpse the eye-popping castle guarding the town), I marched into an open gate with an audible "dong".

It was metal. My head slammed into it. The pain was immediate and excruciating. Blood started flowing. Two gardeners, prostrate on their carpet-like sward, jumped up in alarm. Although they had noticed I was that bloke off the telly, they had been quite discreet about it until I hurled myself into a solid object with unexpected force. They gave an audible gasp.

"Are you alright?" one asked.

He meant my mental state. How could anybody walk into a 10-foot high black tubular metal gate of their own volition? You know, just *march* into it. I am accustomed to being seen as a ninny by the practical classes. I was a representative of the imbecilic celebrity type now. Only a twat off the telly could do anything so naff.

I was doubly hurt. I was in pain and embarrassed. And I was certainly no longer Welsh. I had reverted to "nurture not nature". I was behaving like an English berk, who, on losing a leg in a tragic, limb-severing accident, pretends that nothing has happened. "No, no. I'm fine. Don't make a fuss. Yes I'm quite alright," whilst spurting arterial blood and hopping off to die privately behind a bush.

On this National Trust property (they own bridges too), I merely throbbed and staggered about a bit. But it was symbolic of my visit to the land around Conwy. I was always gawping and never concentrating. There is a lot to see and marvel at. But don't walk into any gates while doing it.

## – PREVIOUS FORM –

Conwy was miles ahead. I began in my own past. I hoped this jaunt to north Wales was going to join up the dots for me. I had been in the region in bits and pieces. I had never bothered to study any maps. Now I hoped to see the whole picture.

Come to think of it, I think I must have done Llandudno with *Top of the Form*, in my scoop-neck sweater days in 1976. I recalled walking on the fine pier and taking a funicular. I was twenty-four and worked for BBC Radio. But I had no recollection of anything more other than that Llandudno was the "Queen of Welsh resorts" or the "Naples of the North" and it is the largest seaside resort in Wales. (And a few other "Top of the Form" facts.)

Thirty years later, I returned to the region, to Betws-y-Coed, with BBC's *Mountain*. Did I spell that correctly? The Betws-y-Coed tourist website found that there were 364 misspellings of the name of the town by people searching for the website, including variations like 'Betsy Cowed' to 'Bwtsy Code'. Anyway, we had been based there for days, heading off for Snowdon and buying fluorescent adventure gear in order to look silly on the train up to the summit.

I had also gone to the Conwy valley with *Restoration*, and had looked at Gwydir Castle and its amazing sitting room walls. But as I passed through each of these places at the behest of a BBC remit (each of the projects mentioned was required to "do" a programme in Wales), I had marvelled at the scenery. I remember phoning my wife with great excitement and telling her that the Conwy valley was exactly like the Rhine, with hummocks of green hills on either side of a river clothed in woods and meadows. This was a little rich. I have never been to the Rhine, but clearly I felt a great affinity with this place. And then, thanks to *Who Do You Think You Are?* in 2010, I discovered that my great, great-grandfather on my father's side had come from Penmachno, just a little further into Snowdonia.

So that was it. I was coming home. Ah.

### – A LIGHTHOUSE IN DISGUISE –

Llandudno sits between two rocky outcrops of land, the Great Orme and the Little Orme. I began my journey on the Great Orme, which was named by the Vikings. (You can get at the original Viking sound if you pucker up the mouth and try your "Norwegian chef" accent: "Orrme" easily metamorphoses into "worrrm".)

It does resemble a mammoth sea slug curled up on itself. I doubt that the Vikings were ever really menaced by huge sea worms, except

# GREAT ORME

THE TOLL HOUSE TO GET ON TO GREAT ORME HAS STOOD SINCE 1878. WHEN IT OPENED IT COST 1D FOR A HORSE AND CARRIAGE TO GO ALONG THE FOUR AND A HALF MILE MARINE DRIVE. TODAY IT COSTS £2.50.

---

IT HAS BEEN ESTIMATED THAT 1,800 TONNES OF COPPER ORE WERE LIFTED OUT OF THE GREAT ORME BY THE PREHISTORIC BRITONS.

---

GREAT ORME IS THE ONLY BRONZE AGE COPPER MINE IN THE WORLD OPEN TO THE PUBLIC.

---

IN 1872 THE SON OF FAMOUS PHOTOGRAPHER WILLIAM SYLVESTER LAROCHE SET UP A PHOTOGRAPHIC STUDIO IN THE OLD QUARRY ON GREAT ORME.

---

THE GREAT ORME TRAMWAY IS THE ONLY CABLE-HAULED TRAMWAY STILL OPERATING ON BRITISH PUBLIC ROADS.

in their imaginations, but I suspect that coming across the bay in a fog this gigantic limestone rock looked terrifying. It's a wildish, winding, smoothed-out place, especially up top, where a herd of Kashmiri goats ramble about the grassland. A supposed gift from Queen Victoria, all 160 of them are said to descend on Llandudno in bad weather and skulk about the streets – like displaced tourists looking for the cinema.

We started in the lighthouse on the tip of the headland. It is now a bed and breakfast. I had to throw a charming Australian woman out of her digs. She was visiting her ancestral home and staying overnight in the lamp room but we needed this glass house, banged onto the front of the fortress, for our filming. The original landowner seems to have been the only romantic in history who found lighthouses disfiguring, and so in 1862 he disguised it as castle, with a "conservatory" strapped on the side where the light sat. This was where I found my "challenge". I was ordered to "find a Welsh dresser".

The castle was a cosy place to holiday in. It must have been for the keepers too. The corridor was lined in planked wood like a boat, and it was decorated with posters from the Mersey Harbour Authority. They seemed to have had an appealing no-nonsense attitude to their business. "Danger. Do not enter," one read. "If not drowned you will be prosecuted." But there were no dressers there for me to examine.

I set off for Llandudno, on a coach. It was a lovely veteran coach. It was painted with a chestnut coloured stripe and covered with chrome. It undertook a recurring trip around the Great Orme. Jon, the driver, kept up a commentary, pointing out the theatre that had burned down, the tollgate to enter (which when it first opened had cost 1p for a horse and carriage), the windfarm in the bay and the lighthouse bed and breakfast, where it stopped to pick me up.

As we rumbled around the headland and across the surprisingly narrow neck of the Great Orme into Llandudno itself, I decided I had better quiz my fellow passengers. "I have been tasked with finding some proper Welsh furniture," I explained to a sweet old lady with white hair. (Probably younger than me.) "Do you have any inherited furniture?"

She looked blank. "No, I don't have any old furniture at all," she said.

I asked the others. They shook their heads. I had assumed it was universally Welsh to hang on to heavy oak bits from old farmhouse ancestors. Perhaps it was just me.

"Jon," I called up the bus. "Can you take her on a long route?"

"The four-and-a-half mile Marine Drive road we had just taken was used as the climax of the 2013 Welsh Rally GB", Jon told us on his public address system, but it wasn't long enough for me; I needed longer.

The coach dutifully swung off along another avenue of suburban seaside villas. As we passed the Llandudno lifeboat station, Jon told us that it is the only lifeboat station in the UK to have its boathouse located in the middle of the town. (It was built in 1861 and positioned there so that it was equidistant from each of Llandudno's main shores.) Meanwhile, I was stalking the aisle like a witless terrorist demanding that the poor tourists identify their racial origins. They cowered away in their plush seats, denying Welsh connections, day-trippers from Walsall or the Wirral all, except for a couple at the back.

"I have a spinning wheel," one woman finally told me. "It's up on a shelf."

"Did you inherit it?" I asked.

"It came from a junk shop. But you won't find a lot of antique stuff in Llandudno. We are far too sophisticated for that." She gave a merry laugh.

A man on the other side of the aisle laughed too. "You might find some antique shops up in the valleys, in countryside beyond the front," he told me.

We eventually parked up just near the pier and I walked off along the prom. It was just after the school holidays had finished but it was still busy. Thousands of white-haired visitors were enjoying the sunny gentility. Eventually I joined a few still sitting out on deck chairs. They were not facing the sea, but had turned towards the town and the slanting sun beaming over the slate roofs of this perfectly preserved Queen of Resorts.

Hired deck chairs were the only thing you could pay for along the entire bay. "There are strict rules," my attendant told me. "Nobody can sell candy floss, or rock, or kiss-me-quick hats on this prom."

Llandudno is autocratic. It is still largely owned by the Mostyn family, who, having decided that sea-bathing could replace mussel-fishing on their beach, purpose-built most of Llandudno in the 1870s. They were so successful that Bismarck and Gladstone came to stay. Other British Prime Ministers followed (if only to bore everybody at conference time). Queen Elisabeth of Romania set up shop in the local hotel. Streets were named after her literary pseudonym: "Carmen Sylva". She went to the Bangor Eisteddfod and watched a classic Punch and Judy show. Lewis Carroll came and met Alice Liddell, widely believed to be the inspiration behind the fictional Alice. Unlike Rhyl and Prestatyn, further along the coast and therefore closer to the great cities of northern England,

Llandudno was up itself. It thought of itself as better than the average and, as a result, it was.

There is nothing particularly dramatic about the wide, grid-like streets. They largely remain as they were intended to be: would-be-uniform terraced houses occasionally sporting the flamboyance of national seaside frivolity, mostly in wrought iron. There may be "iconic" buildings and listed "architectural gems", like the Grand Hotel, which, when opened in 1901, was the biggest hotel in the whole of Wales, but the secret of the place is its uniformity.

Unlike so many fading British seaside towns, there is no evidence of council panic; no one has swept away a dilapidated front to build more accessible car parks or huge leisure centres (though something ominous seems to be going up in the unexpected swathe of green fields that still close the bay on the eastern side). Llandudno is unmodernised.

"We have people all year round these days," Jon the coach driver had told me. "They used to stop coming when the summer finished, but now we are a destination."

And not a destination ruined by its own commerciality. The shops are shops. Llandudno has no mammoth retail centre that becomes deserted at night. Inhabited houses stand shoulder to shoulder with the commercial premises.

In the widespread loss of confidence that followed the package holiday boom, few British seaside towns have shown a matching confidence. Everybody I talked to in Llandudno was in favour of this. That's why they were there, and using the place. Welsh seaside, when it is good, is the best in Britain.

## – WELSH OAK –

My challenge on this visit was to find "a beautiful Welsh dresser". There were side issues to this furniture hunt. I hoped it would get me close to woods and woodcraft. There were questions to be answered. Why was every dresser of note called a Welsh dresser? What was a dresser anyway? Was there anything particular about dressers in this region? And why were the Welsh so obsessed with furniture?

Perhaps it was just my family. I had used Jan Morris as my guide

# LLANDUDNO

LLANDUDNO WAS ORIGINALLY GOING TO
BE CALLED 'PORT WREXHAM'.

---

THE DESIGN OF THE PIER IS UNUSUAL IN
THAT INSTEAD OF A NORMAL STRAIGHT NECK
PROJECTING FROM THE SHORE, LLANDUDNO PIER
HAS A 45-DEGREE TURN ROUGHLY A THIRD
OF THE WAY ALONG ITS LENGTH.

---

MODERN LLANDUDNO TAKES ITS NAME FROM
THE ANCIENT PARISH OF SAINT TUDNO BUT
ALSO ENCOMPASSES SEVERAL NEIGHBOURING
TOWNSHIPS AND DISTRICTS INCLUDING
CRAIG-Y-DON, LLANRHOS AND PENRHYN BAY.

---

THE CAMERA OBSCURA IN LLANDUDNO IS ONE OF
ONLY SEVEN SURVIVING EXAMPLES IN BRITAIN.

---

THERE ARE THE REMAINS OF OVER 30 WRECKED
SHIPS IN LLANDUDNO BAY, ONE OF WHICH
IS A WARSHIP CALLED 'THE PHOENIX' THAT WAS
WRECKED IN 1642.

---

DURING WWI, IN AUGUST 1915, TWO GERMAN
SUBMARINES WERE IN THE WATERS BY LLANDUDNO.
THEY WERE THERE TO RENDEZVOUS WITH THREE
GERMAN OFFICERS WHO ESCAPED FROM A PRISON
CAMP IN LLANSANNAN.

---

IN 1963 THE BEATLES HAD A SIX NIGHT STAY
IN LLANDUDNO WHERE THEY PERFORMED
IN THE LLANDUDNO ODEON.

to Welsh obsessions. I had been ticking them off. She mentioned Welsh dogs, and extreme Welsh weather, Welsh doctors (and my family were mainly doctors or, at least, aspiring doctors) education (that's how they became doctors), mining, rugby, even Welsh nude-bathing, but she left out a Welsh obsession with furniture. In my family, you never inherited money, you inherited huge immovable lumps of oak.

"Ah, that's the court cupboard from your Nain's side," I was told about the yellow oak chest-on-chest with the diamond bone escutcheons. It stood in the corner of the living room. I have it now. (It's handsome but no more a "court cupboard" than my Habitat coffee table.)

I cherish my uncle's "Prince of Wales" cupboard too. "He will want you to have that," my Aunty Megan said to me confidentially, some 30 years ago, with a slight touch of envy in her voice. It was one of the family's group-owned possessions. But I was the one with the family's group-owned pretentions. It would need a "good home". It's in my hallway and it is glass-fronted and surmounted by "feathers"; though I doubt that they have anything to do with the Prince of Wales. They are just carved feathers.

They do come from way back, though, like "the coffer". This is a sturdy, black, immensely heavy, five-foot high trunk, with ogee-arched panelling, and a top section that is split and hinged into doors. It was where the gin-and-tonic glasses were stashed in my childhood. It was passed on to me only a short while ago, via my sister, and now sits in my brother's garage, waiting for me to find the space to accommodate its massive bulk.

The black oak dresser with the dodgy plate rack ("It's not authentic. It was cobbled up from another piece"), the long-case clock and the chairs ("That came from Nain") are all part of the Jones' estate. But I know that most of them originated up north here somewhere, because that's where Nain and Taid (grandmother and father) hailed from.

It wasn't just my family though. Throughout Welsh history, furniture – especially the dresser – was a significant investment, often forming part of a dowry. The National Museum of Wales sums up its importance: "A Welsh dresser is like a personal museum, a place to display old and new, side by side. Things are added and changed, others stay the same through the generations. Each dresser tells the story of its owners."

Hm. A never-ending story, too. But clearly there was nothing of the kind in Llandudno. I would have to go further into the backwoods in search of furniture-fixated farming folk.

Up by the icy-blue lido, to the east of Llandudno, I hitched a lift aboard a passing motorcycle and we roared off up the valley in search of wood.

It was great. This is well-known biker country. I was aware of that because of the many little yellow signs on the roadside that warned me to be aware. "Think bike," they said – not really a happy congruence. It's visceral not cerebral. You can see the point. Empty roads swoop like a switchback. I had joined a convoy of Triumphs. We set off to the fairground.

When you ride pillion, don't lean counter to the centrifugal force, otherwise your gravitational weight will press the bike further over in the bends. Don't put your hand on your partner's bum, either. This much I knew. I hung on wherever I could, leaned into the surges, and we roared off. Pillion is an intimate seating arrangement, but I find it mentally upsetting. I don't like the notion that you really must hold on tight to prevent yourself flying away to your death. Half of me wonders what would happen if I didn't. Or couldn't.

I did though. It's a self-preservation thing. They dropped me off without incident in the depths of old Denbighshire. It was an enjoyable ride. I was grateful.

But that night, walking into the hills, I stood in a glorious late afternoon sun, with the silhouetted humpback of the great tomb of Snowdon fading into blue in the west and at that moment another (unconnected) motorcycle took a road far up the valley to the south. It roared down alongside the river heading for the coast. It was miles away, but we were completely aware of it. Its whining engine reached a painful, jarring, tooth-numbing crescendo, totally audible to the entire region, before coming to another bend, changing down and starting all over again.

On and on it went. Fading a little as it took a dip and then re-emerging with aching clarity. I had to stand, wait and listen while it reduced the valley and destroyed my evening. We wanted to record a lovely, soothing erudite and mawkish piece to camera. So, yes, I was self-interested and, yes, I was partial. But I stood waiting with the cameraman while this monstrous machine rented the evening air for ten minutes. I thought bike. I was aware of bike. And yes, I hated the bloody thing.

# – OAK TREE –

Simon's house was filled with wooden objects. I noticed the heavy oak dining table and the curve-backed wooden chairs. There were wooden sculptures in the garden, wooden bowls on the mantelpieces, wooden kitchen cupboards and wooden benches against the wall. He probably ate with wooden spoons and drove a wooden car.

Simon has eight children, all of whom, boy or girl, have been taught wood-craft and entered competitions with him. Simon himself organised a yearly festival of wood skills called "Woodfest", including felling, lopping, chopping and carving as well as standard carpentry. He ran a business making green oak buildings. In fact, when we had finished he gave me a pintle as a present.

It's an oak nail; made to be knocked into a hole, to hold a joint between beams. Slightly tapered and about eight inches long, it had been cut to shape by hand and it had a satisfying heft. It was an object that everybody would have once taken for granted. Carpentry is becoming a specialised and rare skill. I felt absurdly privileged to be given a whittled stick.

Simon and I were off to look at an asset standing in a field. It was an oak tree. There are 43,000 hectares of oak tree in Wales and 223,000 in Great Britain, accounting for nearly 10 percent of all trees in the country. The English may have hearts of oak like their ships, but we Welsh go one better. We have balls of oak. We have holy trees, magic trees and haunted trees. The word "druid" means "man of the oak". Some claim it derives from the Greek word *drus* (oak). And Wales has a lot of wild and dramatic woods clothing its upland regions.

Looking about in Conwy, one can easily imagine the great wild wood that it is said once covered the whole of Britain. In the prehistoric period this was got out of the way. It has been estimated that most of this was done by the end of the Iron Age, before the birth of Christ, in the first few thousand years of human occupation after the ice age. What is not clear is how they did it. People once assumed that they used fire. But anybody familiar with oak knows that it does not burn easily, hence its use in buildings.

After that, woods, spinneys, copses, closes and thickets thrived on "difficult" ground. Our ancestors needed wood for their fuel and their buildings and they harvested, guarded and cultivated their woodland, particularly in steep, boggy or infertile areas – like Welsh valley hillsides.

This is difficult for a conservationist to say, but almost any building might be reproduced or rebuilt in the space of 12 months, whilst a great oak tree spends 200 years growing, 200 years in its prime and 200 years dying. Ancient trees are the most irreplaceable of objects in our landscape.

And yet, before we get overly romantic about them and start talking of sustainability and green issues, we should also remember that they also serve themselves. Trees reproduce like buggery. There are more of them now than there were in Roman times. Today 12 percent of the country's landmass is covered with forests, accounting for 3,000,000 hectares, 300,000 of which are in Wales.

Oak is the stuff that made the furniture that was part of the Welsh farmhouse. I needed to get closer to that and that was where Simon was taking me. But not too close.

## – WOOD CHOPPER –

Simon opened a gate and led me into a field of cows. I am nervous around cattle, having read lurid accounts of moo-cows losing it on public footpaths, but Simon pushed on, a chainsaw and various bottles of oil in his hands. I followed cautiously. He had given me a couple of steel wedges and a sledgehammer.

"Don't mind this lot," he said, almost barging the cattle out of the way. "They get anxious if you separate them from the calves, but there aren't any calves here."

The cows, however, were distinctly curious. I hurried nervously after him and they followed, towards the centre of the pasture where a skeletal giant stood grey and gaunt against a blue late summer sky. This oak was clearly dead. Not a leaf on it. We frequently see oaks and especially freestanding oaks with a little die-back in their crowns. This is not a new, imported Euro-disease. Shakespeare talks of "stag-headed oaks". But it might mean that the tree is ailing. A mature oak drinks 50 gallons of water a day.

Simon laid down his saw and started inspecting his quarry. He needed to get it to fall where he wanted, and this was a massive trunk with a splayed head of twisted open branches.

Large oak trees are common in this region of Wales, and one of the largest oak trees in the United Kingdom was to be found in Chirk, near Wrexham. It dated back 1,200 years but was toppled in April 2013 by

60-mile-an-hour winds.

Simon pointed to a tussock amongst many tussocks. "The top will come down here," he said decisively, and walked away. These were the complicated logistics of his job. And he had to deal with these inquisitive cows too. I felt for them. I thought cows were sedentary, ruminant, indifferent: the embodiment of calm placidity. This lot shouldered each other aside to get closer to the action. Some began sniffing at the discarded diesel can. Others inspected the sledgehammer.

"They'll all get out of the way once I start up the saw," Simon said confidently.

All around us, rich fields were baking in the sun. Expensive fields too. Some were fetching 12,000 pounds an acre. These valleys had always been a wealthy farming area. Funnily enough it was not an area of great rainfall, lying as it did in the shadow of the great ranges of Snowdonia. In fact, Colwyn Bay regularly holds the title for the hottest place in Wales due to the warm winds that develop over Snowdon. But the region still supports mixed farming. As a result there are bushy hedges and verdant woods, crops of maize corn and wheat and, of course, cows.

Simon started his chainsaw – his precision tool. The cows jumped a bit, but they certainly didn't run away. After an initial mild lowing, and an orchestrated shuffle, they regrouped quickly.

Simon was indeed a tree-surgeon. I was expecting a steady, contemplative, approach. After all, the camera was running. Surely he would cut a bit, stand, scratch his head and contemplate, but he moved quickly, like a man in a hurry.

With several quick swings, he sliced off "the buttresses". These are the rounded corners at the base of the trunk where it splays off to meet the big roots. The chainsaw sliced like a scalpel. One cut in, like a cheese, one cut down, and parabolic sections fell away. He quickly showed me how the rotten soft wood of the external surface was only a few inches deep. This was a good sign. It meant that the heart-wood was solid. And then he was off again.

Several heifers began a detailed and concentrated examination of the discarded wood. Meanwhile Simon was busying himself around the back of the tree, on the up-side, away from the fall path, cutting out a wedge, which was similarly discarded. This was followed by a single deep cut into the middle of the gouged bit. I was invited to step forward and make my contribution. The two steel wedges were already rammed into the cut.

"Go on, then."

I knocked them home with the sledgehammer.

"I think that will probably be enough," Simon said. "Sometimes I need to do more, but we have set up the tension. That should do the work for us."

He now worked out of my vision at the front. I was tempted to step forward but too close an inspection on that side might be a little foolhardy. This was his magic bit. Only the sound of the saw kept the cows at a respectful distance. After a few deft strokes he was back and now ready for the final blow.

"OK?" he said.

I nodded. I was fine.

He leaned in, sawed for a few seconds and stood back. There was no creak. There was no shudder. The great trunk simply toppled, as if of its own volition, but, in fact, pushed over by the "tension" set up by those two small wedges in the stern cut.

Most of the cows stood back attentively in a row just beyond the fall-line. A lone black steer seemed to realise it was a little too close, paused and then shimmied nonchalantly away at the last moment.

The tree hit the field with a cracking roar. It scattered rotten branches and bark like a wreck. There was a pause. The cows looked on and then, jostling each other out of the way in their eagerness, came forward to sniff its carcass and taste its bark. This was distinctly odd. The tree was the same tree that had until a few moments ago been standing upright in their field. None of them seemed to have any interest in it then.

Close up, the upper branches were white and rotten. I could easily break off big limbs with a twist of the wrist. Yet the core of the trunk was sound. It would make wide planks and heavy timber after seasoning. Now it had to be stored and dried for two years before it could properly be used. The rest, at the top, could go for kindling or bark mulch. The forestry industry is important in Wales; it contributes more than £340 million per annum to the Welsh economy.

"So tell me Simon, how much is this tree worth?" I asked.

"In its current state?" He looked it up and down, as if estimating the amount of useable timber that might be extracted. "About £2,000."

The tree had probably been growing for about three hundred years.

# – UP YOUR DOUGLAS FIR –

I was surprised by the value of our felled oak. I thought it would have been worth more. But there was still work to be done and a long time to wait before it could become useable. This is one of the reasons why forestry people can't be bothered with broadleafed trees. Oaks, ash, elm, beech – our native species – all take time to grow. The quick return comes with pine, and the best way to get that return is to plant soft wood like a crop and the way to do that is to plant it in serried ranks and the effect of this is to make a series of ugly slab-like wodges on the landscape.

When a group of celebrities recently stepped forward to prevent the selling off of "our" forests, I suspect they imagined they were saving mighty beeches and oaks. In fact they were largely preserving a curious system of state-backed, redundant monoculture, introduced after the First World War. The submarine blockade stopped cargoes of wood reaching Britain. The country needed pit-props and matches. So in the 1920s a government institution was formed that planted geometric, dark plantations across our uplands. These woods are not just aesthetically intrusive, they are environmentally destructive too, producing acid water run-off and destroying natural habitat. Had they planted mixed woodlands in well-planned batches that clothed the hills, the tourist industry and the spiritual good of everybody would have benefited greatly. And we would have had supplies of renewable strong timber. Now they don't know what to do with much of their pulp-chipboard stuff.

On the side of a steep hill where a landowner had planted a stand of Douglas fir to provide emergency pit-props for an industry that no longer needs such things, an ex-marine has finally found another use for them. He has built a tree-top training circuit.

The towering pines stand on a steep slope. Douglas firs are known for their height; indeed the tallest tree in Wales used to be a Douglas fir standing at 60 metres tall in a forest in Powys. I climbed a ladder and got myself up onto a platform. A series of interlinking bridges, ropes and beams took a level route away through the uniform field of trunks. The first platform was not very high. This was cunning. It gave a false sense of limited insecurity.

Having been strapped into a safety harness (with a line on my back attached to a wire, to hold me from falling a few feet, no great distance anyway), I clumsily followed a bunch of twelve year olds as they scampered across the beam, swung out on a rope and skipped across a swinging, battened bridge. They went at agitated lemur speed. I was the sloth. I clambered after them, hanging on to every handhold with a steely grip, and very slowly wobbling across a prostrate log. It was a small circuit and it brought me back to where I had started. Not too demanding. This was clever.

It was just a test: a mere trial. The real course set off in another direction altogether. Any guidance I might have got from those in front of me disappeared with a giggle and a patter of training shoes somewhere in the gloom of the trunks ahead. I turned. The boy following me was looking resigned. He couldn't overtake. He was doomed to follow a terrified old man who had lost his sense of balance. He had to wait as this feeble, cautious, cowardly, cack-handed, hesitant, weak-kneed crock wobbled his way across the course.

It was ghastly. I knew I was tied on. I knew that a slip would have merely resulted in an uncomfortable wallop to an undignified trussing, but my brain didn't appreciate that. Each step felt entirely wrong. And there were some complicated steps.

There was the row of hanging tyres. I had to place each foot in one loosely dangling tyre after another and step across. There was the slack rope, with just two dangling bits of string with which to support myself. There was the straight narrow beam that I had to cross like a tightrope. There was the row of free swinging logs. These were in the horizontal position, and then, wait a minute, the row of free swinging logs in the vertical position. And then… How long was this course?

There were an estimated 86,000,000 visits to woodlands in Wales in 2011, and walking was the main activity undertaken by these visitors. None of them walked as slowly as me and I began to realise that the obstacles ahead stretched away to the crack of doom, somewhere on the other side of the plantation. Each stage was taking me about 10 minutes.

The little boy behind me was looking increasingly rueful. Each obstacle was getting higher. Or rather, the ground was getting further away, because we were effectively traversing out across the slope and by now the ground was 30 feet below and the slack wires that had to be negotiated were slacker.

Jason the ex-marine was standing way below me. His massive hams of shoulders had become mere quail legs surmounted by a shaven pimple. This was his head from which emanated advice. "Lean out!!" he called.

Lean out? I couldn't release the hold on the branch I was next to. If you ever wondered whether you were a tree-hugger, try this assault course. You will embrace trees far more fervently than you have ever hugged your children. Never has a warm, red, fat trunk seemed so comforting and cosy.

"Reach out for the next rope beyond!!" That was another favourite instruction, hollered up from somewhere in the void, and not bad advice when the grip on the rope I had in my hand was faltering so badly.

"I think I may be having a heart attack."

"No, no, you're doing fine!"

Well, what the hell did he know? Jason was barely visible now. And I wasn't going to look down anyway.

I had the presence of mind, if not to bleat, then at the least to address my director in a hollow tone. "I do think we have probably got enough of this by now," I croaked.

"Oh yes, undoubtedly," Chris shouted back.

"Shall I come down?"

"There's no way down," Jason shouted. "You have to go on to the end to get down."

"You are quite right, though," Chris shouted. "We'll get the camera up to the end. Hang on there."

This was a fairly redundant instruction. I was hanging already. Whether I could sustain my dangling was mere conjecture on his part. I pressed on, with the lemur behind me skipping across in seconds, and finally, after three impossible bridges and two suicidal ones, I reached a final platform high in the upper branches of a straight Douglas fir that was now swaying perceptibly in the breeze.

Francesca, the course instructor, was waiting for me. She could have taken a course in advanced astrophysics and a PhD while she did so. "OK. So the way down is very quick," she explained. We were standing on a minute wooden platform. "I am just attaching this cable to your harness. You can't feel it but it comes into action as you fall and slows your descent."

"What descent?"

"You just have to step off."

I looked down. The forest floor was a long way below. This was a demanding "step". A number of people were looking up at me. They were barely discernible.

"I'm not sure I can."

"Yes, it's easy," said Francesca firmly.

I intrinsically believed her. My operational intelligence understood that this well-respected tourist attraction would be shut down if their automatic descent-arresting wire failed on a regular basis. But my body was now beyond rationality. I was required to step off into the void. I couldn't do it. I have lowered myself off skyscrapers, climbed north faces and abseiled down ventilation shafts, all in the name of television "jeopardy", but this was one small step for a man and one giant step for an abject coward. Not since the top board at High Beech swimming pool at the age of eight had I felt so challenged in my bowels.

And then from some 60 feet I sensed a growing impatience somewhere down below. Well, bugger that. I went.

I don't believe Butch Cassidy and the Sundance Kid. Or that "Geronimo!" stuff. I didn't make a great whoop. I might have whimpered. I walked off like a man on the scaffold. Whoosh. Clunk. And I fell to my instant death.

Er… no. In truth, I whizzed down to land perfectly safely just like everybody else. An unseen hand grabbed me from behind and slowed my descent. Not so slow, however, that I didn't feel an appreciable jar when I hit the ground. I forgot to bend my knees.

Jason slapped me on the back. But, as I smiled weakly and nodded pathetically, in my peripheral vision I could just make out that six year old who had followed me. He was giving me a surprisingly adult look.

## – ANTIQUE SHOPS –

The village of Llangernyw straddles the main A548 between Llanrwst and Llanfair Talhaiarn. There's a church and a big, busy pub, a tiny shop and a few houses scattered at the crossroads. The river Elwy glides through quietly and the road noisily. I was there to look at another tree, but as I passed I noticed that there was an unusually discreet antique shop tucked a little way up the southern road. At last, some chance of making contact with north Walian furniture. I was almost trembling as I pushed the door open.

It was a small room and a crowded one. A good moment, when the gloom settles and the eye ranges around: a quick assessment followed by a longer careful trawl.

Perhaps the real antiques have all gone by now. These days junk seems to get offloaded from an Eastern Europe Euro-Antique frontier. Beaten-up, wormy, crudely-painted boxes that look as if they might have been for the house pig are stacked on tables with oddly short legs, sawn down because the bottoms had rotted away with endless sluicing of some hovel's floor.

What I was looking for is called "country furniture" by the trade: the plainer the better. I was seeking straightforward Welsh objects made with good oak or fruitwood, with a strong, warm colour acquired over many years.

It would be heavy; if there was imperfection, so much the better. One of the experts we spoke to about Welsh dressers told us that you can often tell if a dresser is authentic by the back panelling. When they were first made, craftsmen used any scrap of wood they could get and, as such, the panels were not uniform. Mass production of course changed all this and many back panels were replaced with new mass-produced planks as damp cottage and farmhouse walls rotted the wood over the years.

I doubt very much that the average Welsh farmhouse was furnished to look like "World of Interiors", with beautiful spare pieces in a shaft of light on a worn stone floor. Photographs taken at the beginning of the twentieth-century show kitchens that look like chaotic, dirty pubs. Hundreds of jugs hang from the ceiling and wild, gap-toothed inhabitants are crouched down amongst highly polished pieces of copper in dark, almost black caves. The furniture can barely be glimpsed in the gloom. And yet they had it. And they bought it locally.

Here in Llangernyw, I immediately noticed that there was no dresser on display. I was struck, however, by two eighteenth-century, long-case clocks, sometimes called "grandfather clocks". They were standing against the wall. The usual cumbersome large "head" holding the clock-face was balanced on a coffin-sized box, with a door in front, where the pendulum swung.

I knew the type well, because, naturally enough, we have a similar one in my family. It is in my Pembrokeshire dining room. My mother had presented it to me with the usual forceful ritual. It came from my father's "side" and bore the legend "Cardigan" on its decorated face. I was proud to have it in Wales. Like myself, it had come home. After all, Cardigan was only 25 miles from my little farmhouse.

I peered closely at the face of the clock in the shop. It had "Llanrwst" painted on it. "That's close to here, isn't it?" I asked.

"Oh yes," said Bethan, the owner, from behind her counter, barricaded into the corner by stacked furniture. "It's the next village up the road."

I was impressed. "And the other one?"

"That's from Abergele. Just down the other way."

This was truly local. Here were two pieces of relatively complicated furniture, the same basic idea, but with individual and identifiable personal variations, made within a few miles of where I was standing.

"So did you go to auctions to retrieve these and bring them back to the district?" I asked.

"Oh no." She seemed amused by the notion. "They both came from local farmhouses."

Bethan and her husband, who repaired the stuff they sold, rarely visited auctions and certainly never got on the road to go trawling through Romanian or Montpellier markets. Both of the clocks came from local families who had passed them down by inheritance and now found that they really had no need or perhaps space for them. Bethan had been asked to sell them. She acquired all her stock by similar methods.

I was excited. This was the vindication of the Welsh furniture story. Not only were the pieces proper heirlooms, which had stayed and been polished in the locality, they were made by local cabinet-makers.

"There were seven clockmakers at one time in Llanrwst," Bethan pointed out. It was a tiny place. "There was one in this village too." Llangernyw was even tinier.

We speculated on how the system worked. They had probably sent off to Birmingham for the clock mechanism, which was painted up in some little slum factory. Perhaps that factory provided, as a service, the name of the village of origin under the views of castles or roses (or, for the more elaborate mechanisms, entire seascapes with square rigged ships flying flags under rotating mechanical moons.) The local man then sawed the planks of oak and constructed the case. And of course every modern, model farmhouse, with staff to set to work and cows to milk, needed a clock in their parlour.

They probably needed a fine heavy "coffer" or chest to keep blankets in too. She had one from a local farm. And they might have needed a strong "carver", or well-made armchair, in heavy sawn (not turned) oak. She had one of those. The farmers would have needed a court cupboard, possibly something fine and highly carved. There was one against the back wall, though we both shook our heads over that, because it was a little too refined. There were lustre jugs, which went on shelves to twinkle in the fire and Staffordshire dogs, often won at fairs (and called fairings as a result) which would have added to the shiny clutter. All these things I noted and rather wanted, but there wasn't any sign of that other staple, the dresser.

"Oh, we do get them," said Bethan, reassuringly, implying that, if I just hung around for a few years, some nearby family would tire of theirs and call her in.

She didn't really want to discuss prices. It was a bad time. Five years before, the market had been strong, but during the recession it had collapsed. In truth she wondered whether the demand would ever come back. Black oak was not as fashionable as it had been. Most people weren't trying to fake up a romantic olde-worlde atmosphere like me. They prefowed wipe-clean Ikea. She was perfectly aware, though, that there were still collectors who honed in on really good items. And I knew what she meant. The authentic, sturdily-made piece of country furniture is a lovesome thing. I have no doubt that when Bethan gets her dresser it will be the real thing. But I didn't have years to wait.

## – YEW OR NON-YEW –

I crossed the road to the churchyard of St Digain's. I knew what I was looking for. Tommy Cooper (yes, that really was his name), the gardener, was sitting on a grave and pointed the way. "It's over there," he said. "You know originally there was no fuss about it at all." He went on. "It was all covered with brambles and nettles in that corner but we've cleared them away now."

I looked across at a large, but not specifically giant, yew tree.

"An expert told us that it was 4,000 years old, but other experts disputed that and came down to have a look. They decided it was 4,800 years old. And so they settled on 4,500."

I walked over to the tree and then through it. The thing itself is a group of limbs now, as many ancient trees are. It looked as if it had sprouted from a stool or pollarded trunk. I was just guessing. Experts would undoubtedly point out that it was never "harvested" as a pollarded tree would have been. It was more probable that the central trunk had rotted away. It had lost its middle section. The two outer parts, continuing to thrive, had simply divided and branched out into separate trunks. Taken around the whole lot, it now measures more than 10m in circumference, which is part of the method for calculating the age.

Yew has the advantage of being able to fracture and split as branches become too heavy, without diseases infecting the whole of the tree. A gardener making hedges will tell you that fresh growth springs from any cut. As a result this ancient organism appeared to have spread like a splayed hand, and its dense, dark, tiny leaves now shaded a considerable bare patch of earth, grown into a slight mound from many centuries of steadily dropping needles. Evergreens shed dead leaves throughout the year, rather than in the autumn.

Tommy explained that, until they had been alerted to the potential age and status of the tree, the church had kept its oil tank in the middle of it. Rather too many dead branches were cleared away as it was "freshened up", and the loss of these apparently prevented "dendrochronologists" from getting a really accurate measure of its age. But the Tree Council has now named it one of the "50 great trees of Britain".

Viewed close up, the wood twisted and furled like rope. The bark was warm and red and, at the older intersections of the branches, the grain of the tree swirled like melted chocolate. Gazing into these whorls one appreciated the age of the thing. There was something thick, dense and knotty there.

Yew makes great hard furniture with wonderful colour. Otherwise you might have passed by without a second glance: just another yew in a churchyard. A few moments' meditation, however, under the canopy of this ancient living thing invites the making of connections. They say that yews are pagan trees, that they predate Christianity and have connections with ancient holy sites. Julius Caesar noted that the Gauls and other north Europeans committed suicide by taking poison from yews in order to escape his clutches. The oldest wooden object in the world is a spearhead made of yew, found near Clacton in Essex and estimated to be between 350,000 and 450,000 years old. Certainly these grave trees, a symbol of darkness in any churchyard, were part of the ancient world and its mysteries. They remain mysterious. But just the name is tantalising. The Latin countries call it a *Taxus*, but the word we use has some sort of old German origin. The Welsh for yew is *ywen*.

Was this particular great bush here some holy thing which predated the church itself? Was I standing under a tree which had begun to grow around the time that Stonehenge was being erected? Did later Christians simply employ pagan holy trees as sites for places of worship? There is a certificate celebrating the yew's 4,000 years, signed by David Bellamy. Others are more stingy. They assert it is only about 1,000 years old, which might mean that the early Welsh saints planted this tree themselves to dignify their place of worship. Either way, the Llangernyw Yew had seen some history. Nothing more spectacular, I sensed, than the steady passage of the seasons and the quiet pace of a rural enclave, but it invoked awe and contemplation and respect.

## – CONWY TWITTED –

Once I stopped the bleeding I was left with a visible scar on the dome of my forehead. I found the camera crew and we filmed me trudging across the footbridge several times. "Does it show?" I asked Nick.

"What?"

"My wound."

He looked at me and then played film back on the camera. "Yes," he said.

We got hold of some pink, liquid make-up and dabbed it into the cut. I didn't feel this was good for it, but I imagined that make-up had to have some antiseptic precautions. Now, with what appeared to be a loathsome pink skin infection on my brow, we resumed filming and I wandered into Conwy itself.

Shut the gates, town council! Here was a walled town, with some of the finest medieval ramparts in Europe, with fine medieval gates at the quarters, and still a daily chaos of cars and buses pour in, taking a short-cut, the only cut to the bridges across the Conwy River.

Edward I would have done something about it. He was full of rules. He built the castle at the end of the thirteenth century to control the Welsh. Apparently, the fortress was originally whitewashed, which was difficult to imagine as we walked under its black and grey eminence now. Wales is believed to have more castles per square mile than anywhere else in the world. There are over 600 across the country. It is estimated Edward I spent £15,000 building this one in Conwy, the largest sum spent on any of his Welsh castles. No surprise, then, that it's regarded as one of the finest surviving medieval fortifications in Britain. They kept out the locals, who were only allowed in on market day. Perhaps the modern traffic is a revenge for that.

I found my dresser in a clock shop in the upper reaches of the town. It was simple enough, made of oak, with its lower areas enclosed by cupboards. Ken, the owner of the shop, could place it exactly. It came from Anglesey, he told me; so not exactly local-local, but certainly not from far away and definitely, with those cupboards underneath, from north Wales. You see there are distinct differences in Welsh dressers depending on where they were made. In north Wales they were more akin to a cupboard and the traditional image of a Welsh dresser. In the south they were more like a sideboard, while in mid Wales, some were 'crooked', designed to fit into the small corners of workman's cottages. As a result some experts argue that the mid Wales dresser is the true ancestor of the modern fitted kitchen.

Ken pointed down to an empty space on the lower level between the doors to either side of his specimen. "It has a dog kennel here," he said. I was sceptical but he was utterly convincing. "The farmer came in and his tea was on the table and his sheep dog was ordered in there, or that is what I have always been told," he said.

The dresser had a lovely dark colour. How did they get that? I understood you had to be careful of modern furniture polishes and their chemical glazes.

"They used boot polish," Ken told me. "My father kept this shop before me and I was often put to work as a child to polish the tables and it was always plain boot polish. That's what the ladies in the farms used. It made them darker." We admired the colour for a moment. "If you had wanted to buy this dresser five years ago," Ken explained, "it would have been a lot more. The highest price I have heard for a Welsh dresser was paid at an auction in Chester. It was in excess of £45,000."

I was impressed. I have seen some lovely things, but that is lot for a "China hutch", as they call it in the States.

"I believe it was bought by a farmer up by Caernarfon way," Ken continued.

So it hadn't gone to some plutocrat collector in America. A valuable piece of local workmanship had gone back to the sort of place it was made for. Not only was it a lot to pay for a dresser, it was a lot of money for a farmer to have spare. The rich fields that I had passed through on my journey into the hinterland were still generating wealth then, for some at least.

I had fulfilled my quest, but I wasn't going to buy Ken's dresser. I had plenty of family dressers to cope with already. It seemed a perfectly reasonable price. After all, Welsh dressers or any other bits of Welsh furniture, unlike that swimming pool or fitted carpet or that holiday in Bali, represent a wholly moveable investment, don't they? It's a tangible lump you can leave to your children, just as long as they can get hold of a sturdy removal van and find a spare wall, preferably not too damp.

# CONWY

CONWY CASTLE IS CONSIDERED BY
MANY TO BE ONE OF THE GREATEST
ACHIEVEMENTS OF MILITARY
ARCHITECTURE IN THE MIDDLE AGES.

---

IT TOOK OVER 15,000 MEN TO BUILD
CONWY CASTLE AND FOUR YEARS
TO COMPLETE.

---

THE GREAT HALL IN THE CASTLE IS ALMOST
130FT LONG AND THE WALLS FOR THE PRISON
ARE 13FT THICK.

---

ABERCONWY HOUSE IN CONWY IS ONE
OF THE OLDEST HOUSES IN WALES.

---

THE CONWY ROAD TUNNEL WAS THE
FIRST IMMERSED TUBE TUNNEL TO BE
BUILT IN THE UK.

---

CONWY HAS OVER 200 LISTED BUILDINGS
WITHIN ITS WALLS.

---

IN SOME OF THE SANDY BANKS NEAR CONWY
THERE ARE OLD TREE STUMPS THAT ARE THE
REMAINS OF A SUBMERGED FOREST DATING
BACK 7000 YEARS.

After we had finished all my little trips and the television series was off being edited, I was asked to go to the Welsh BAFTAs 2013. A programme I had made a year earlier about a pilgrimage route from Holywell to St Davids had resulted in a nomination: "Best Presenter". Well, well. We'll keep a welcome indeed. As it happens I was off in the South of France on a holiday racing boats and eating prawns but it was considered "politic" to return. After all, what would Welsh telly think if I was standoffish? I wasn't standoffish. I was honoured. I got on a plane and flew back to Bristol. I booked into a Cardiff hotel. I discovered I had lost my bow tie in customs and pinched the one my friend Rob was wearing. He arrived at the Millennium Centre with an open collar, but I had made the effort. I looked like a waiter. Yes, I looked the part. So did the Centre. There was a red carpet leading up to the revolving front door and ranged along it were a sprinkling of "media opportunities": stringers with microphones at half-mast waiting to catch the "slebs". I was almost inside and past the lot before *Buzz*, the Cardiff listing magazine, finally decided to hail me "for a few words". Then BBC Wales decided they had better interview me too. This is the way. One begins and the others follow, dreading going back to their editor minus the scoop that I "dissed Michael Sheen" or whatever they thought I had told the BBC. Finally even S4C right down the other end decided they might as well interview me too.

"So Griff," the interviewer began. "How do you feel about being up against a Welsh presenter?"

This was a difficult question, obviously. The other nominations were Huw Edwards and Aled Sam, S4C's own country and furnishings expert. But I felt bold enough to bat this one away.

"Well, er, the clue is in the name," I began cautiously. "My name is Griffith Rhys Jones. I was born about half a mile from where we are standing. My mother was from the Rhondda, my father from Penylan. Every single one of my relatives, tracing back as far as *Who Do You Think You Are?* were able to go, were Welsh. I think I am Welsh."

"Oh." He stared me down. Not a flicker of distraction crossed his features. Instead, he stopped the recording. "Take it back," he said to his cameraman. "Let's start again." The cameraman fiddled a bit, wobbled his machine up to his shoulder and the microphone was thrust back in my face. "So, Griff, welcome to the BAFTAs," the presenter chirruped anew. "What do you think your chances are against a *proper* Welsh presenter?"

They weren't good. Huw Edwards triumphed, deservedly. I went back to my cosmopolitan lifestyle the following morning. And I guess I do have to accept defeat. I am not a proper Welshman. I know. As I made my way through the splendours of Wales on my multi-journey, mini-odyssey, I realised that despite my inherited cupboards and my Aunty Megans and Gwens, despite my intimate knowledge of Pembrokeshire, and my natural affinity for Corgi dogs, I have missed something essential. I have not spent enough of my life in the Land of My Fathers. I have not absorbed the distinctions of the culture. There are nuances in the language I can never now understand, there are reactions to outsiders I can never share, there are cultural norms that I cannot embrace. I must always remain the outside Welshman, the backdoor Cambrian, the would-be boyo. Never mind. To the vast majority of people I met that didn't matter a jot. They were charming, friendly and warmly welcoming. During October, Arfon from Tacla Taid on Anglesey went to huge efforts to try to get me a Jones bailer, a particularly wonderful toy to go with my Massey Ferguson, on the basis of our few minutes together in his Land Rover series one. This warmth was typical. I saw wonders. I gobbled up the scenery, I ate well, slept well and I learnt a lot: from the ambitions of Edward I to the appetites of the dung beetle. What a country, what variety, what people. In the end I can say that I think I am rather privileged to be a dispossessed Welsh person and a perpetual outsider in Wales. As a result I need take nothing for granted. I still have a lot to master. Good.

# – ACKNOWLEDGEMENT –

Many people helped to get this book together, but I would particularly like to thank Christopher Bruce, Celyn Williams and Scott Dewey for their ideas, Tudor Evans, Nick Manley and Brian Murrell for their backchat, Cat Ledger for her ministrations, Sarah Broughton and Clare Byrne for their steadfastness, Richard Davies and Francesca Rhydderch at Parthian for their professionalism and Jo for her attention and support. And all the people we met and who put up with us too. Diolch yn fawr.

SERIES EDITOR: DAI SMITH

WWW.THELIBRARYOFWALES.COM

# THE LIBRARY
# OF WALES.COM

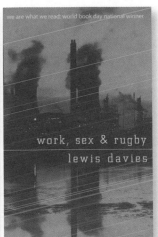
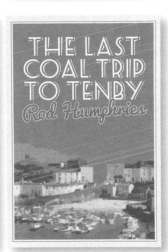

# Wales
# Cymru

## Wales. Famous for its great outdoors.

Views that take your breath away.
Even if the walk doesn't.

visitwales.com